TALES OF THE CESSNA 195

Michael D. Larson

Erie, Colorado

ISBN: 0692281460
ISBN-13: 978-0692281468

This is harder than I thought. So many people have been instrumental in my career as a pilot; I don't know where to start. Well, yes I do.

How many husbands can say their wife is as enthusiastic about their passion as they are. I can. For that, I dedicate this book to the love of my life, my wife of 39 years, Charmian. She and the family we have are probably the only things I ever cared more about than flying.

TABLE OF CONTENTS

1

THE LOVE OF FLYING

In the summer of 1959, I was 12 years old and in Wichita, Kansas visiting family for a few weeks. Dad had driven us from Sioux City, Iowa, to Omaha, Nebraska, and we caught the train to Newton, Kansas. One of my aunts and uncles lived out on the southeast side of Wichita, not far from Pawnee Avenue and the Cessna Aircraft factory. I would sit out in the yard and watch the Cessnas fly from the factory on their test flights and I could identify each and every one of them. One morning I determined that it couldn't be too far to the factory itself so I set out to get a better look at the airplanes. Indeed it was less than a mile to the Pawnee plant and I found a good spot at the end of the runway and decided to spend the rest of the day watching the airplanes. One after another the Cessnas would taxi down and do their run ups, I knew the procedure and watched as they checked each magneto then cycled the constant speed propellers if one was installed. The 182s, 172s, 150s and 210s were steadily parading by and I couldn't believe my luck, I would rather be here watching and learning about these Cessnas than any other place in the world.

A new Cessna 180 ready to be delivered.

As the morning wore on, the July sun rose in the eastern sky but the heat didn't have the slightest effect on my comfort as long as the steady show of Cessna aircraft passed by. After about three hours an unpainted 210 pulled off of the taxi-way, parked on the grass and shut down its engine. As the prop came to a stop the door opened and the pilot in an olive drab flight suit began to walk steadily in my direction. At first I thought my little paradise was about to be taken away from me, this pilot was going to send me home for my own safety. I considered running out of earshot so I could come back after he left, but I stood my ground determined to stay as long as possible, besides, as the gentleman approached a little closer I could see he had a smile on his face. He's a pilot and must know I have some interest here so maybe he'll cut me some slack. As he neared the fence he said, "Hello there, my name is Bill McNeil, what's yours?"

I told him I was Mike Larson and my mom knew where I was. He laughed and explained that he would be flying all day and if I ran home and got a note from mother that said it would be okay to go flying, he would meet me at the factory entrance at noon and give me a ride. I couldn't believe what I was hearing. This gentleman wasn't going to send me away. He was offering me more than I could have hoped for, a ride in one of those beautiful new Cessnas. It didn't take me long to tell him yes sir, "I'll do just that and meet you at noon." I was a half mile away at a full gallop before he made it back to the 210.

I wasn't sure mom was going to agree to write the note, she was terrified of airplanes. As I explained the deal to her I could see in her eyes that she didn't like the idea of giving permission for some stranger to take her 12-year-old son up in an airplane, but she also knew of my passion for flying and I had only been up twice before in my life. Finally, she decided this was one opportunity she could not deny me. With that precious note in hand, I headed back to the factory, determined not to be there one second late.

To my great relief, Bill McNeil was standing at the entrance as I rounded the corner and I was granted entrance to the Promised Land: the Cessna Aircraft Company factory.

I was on cloud nine as Bill escorted me through the different areas of the assembly plant carefully explaining how the aircraft were built and the quality control procedures required to make sure each plane met the strict safety standards required to keep these airplanes the best in the world. He was preaching to the choir, I had already determined the quality of the Cessna airplane while watching them fly by all morning long. I'll never forget the things I saw and smelled and touched that day. Bill patiently strolled though the factory showing me aluminum rolls ready to be cut and riveted onto wings and fuselages and finally to the paint shop where the unique trim designs were added to the final product.

Bill McNeil. Picture taken with my Kodak Brownie camera shortly after landing back at the Cessna Factory.

From the paint shop we began walking towards the flight line where several airplanes were being readied for test flights. My heart raced as we walked toward the same Cessna 210 that

Bill had parked on the grass only a few hours before. Bill began a careful walk around of the airplane and explained everything he was looking at and why they were so important, then he opened the right door and showed me where I would be sitting. Once in, Bill pulled out a check list and began to prepare for flight. Those sensations of starting the engine and taxiing a Cessna airplane are all familiar to me today but, that day, they were all fresh.

Bill McNeill and Mort Brown (Chief Production Test Pilot).

Even today, I remember how excited I was listening to the vibrations from the engine starting, the sound of the gyros spooling up and the radio crackling from the overhead speaker. On takeoff the acceleration took my breath away as I realized that, at last, I'm flying again, but this time it's the real thing, not one of the thousands of day dreams of the past several years. I was finally and at last flying in a real airplane. Bill leveled off a couple of thousand feet up and accelerated to the north of Wichita. I was busy looking at everything all at once, trying to take in as much as I could when Bill tapped me on the shoulder and pointed ahead and to the left. There, only a few miles away, in a sharp left turn was a gorgeous corporate A-26 sailing by. I smiled at the sight and watched him speed away, thinking of how many times I had looked at those babies in *Flying* magazine and how lucky I am to be seeing one from this angle. Now, another tap on the shoulder and Bill is motioning towards the control wheel. I understand immediately that he is offering me the chance to fly and I eagerly placed both hands on the wheel and keep the airplane straight and level. Soon Bill is pointing to the north and I turned the Cessna in that direction and did a few cautious turns. Bill brought back the power and we started a slow descent towards Newton, Kansas, I was surprised we could already be as far as Newton, it seemed to take so long to drive from there a few nights ago. He patiently talked me though the approach to the airport and somehow we got the 210 on the ground without damage and off went back into the air. Even though I still had the wheel in hand I knew Bill was keeping things under control. After about a half hour we touched down back at the factory and taxied back to the flight line. Bill made the appropriate entries into the log book and I watched him sign the aircraft off as airworthy and knew that tomorrow she'll be in the paint shop being readied for her new owner. I couldn't help that I had a giant smile for the rest of the day.

Bill offered to drive me back to Uncle Bill's house and once there he came in for a cup of coffee and that was the start of a long family friendship. We kept in touch by letter and phone for several years. He was always guiding me in the right direction and would never hesitate to offer support and advice while I navigated my teen age years and tried to become a man.

Our 1949 Cessna 195 flying over south Texas.

Bill retired from Cessna in the 1970s and rode motorcycles and drove around in his motor home and beloved Karmann Ghia. He died a few years later. I did not find out about it until my aunt's father was buried in Wichita. One day, while visiting her father's grave, Aunt Mary noticed a Cessna airplane cut into one of the tombstones nearby. She immediately recognized the name, Bill McNeil, as the man who had stopped by for coffee that July afternoon after taking her nephew for a ride.

I can't imagine this happening today. The liability issues probably would keep some kid so far away from the runway he wouldn't waste his time trying to watch the airplanes. I guess that's where EAA's Young Eagle program is so valuable. It's just about the only way a kid can get close to an airplane today. Most airports are so tightly fenced in that even a grown-up can't get close to the real thing. I like to take people for a ride in our beautiful Cessna 195 and I get a special kick out of showing some young person what it is like to fly and how easy the basics are to learn. If they show any interest at all I'll try to make arrangements to take them up in the Cub at a later time so they can really get into the basics. I owe it to these young kids to see if they really want to become pilots. After all, if it hadn't been for Bill McNeil, I might not have been able to enjoy a career devoted to aviation like I have for all of these years. Yes sir, I know Bill, it's my turn!

2

THE TWIN BEECH 18 CHRONICLES

Only a Colorado Saturday morning could be this beautiful. It was the 17th of June, 1972 at Columbine Airport 18 miles southwest of Denver. I was looking forward to another gorgeous weekend of flying parachute jumpers. We had two Cessna 180s and had just bought a Twin Beech. I also thought I might even make one or two jumps this weekend myself. I was one-third owner of Columbine Parachute Center and we were going great guns this summer. Business had been so good we managed to talk our Denver banker into financing the Twin Beech 18 for us. It took a couple of months to find the right Beech and then another three weeks for Combs Aircraft to complete the annual inspection and now we had it at Columbine ready to work. We were fortunate to have mentoring from Jim McKinstry, a United Airlines pilot. Jim looked the old airplane over for us before we bought it and agreed to check me out when the annual was complete. There was one problem; I still didn't have a multi-engine rating. I had my GI bill benefits but there was a delay getting them approved. Now the airplane was ready to work and we needed a pilot in the interim. We knew an ex WASP who owned a Cessna 180 and she had flown Beech 18's and everything else during World War II. Jim gave Gracie a check ride and she was flying the first load this morning while I was at the flight school taking a multi- engine lesson in a Piper Twin Comanche.

I crouched forward and yelled, "CLEAR LEFT" through the little open window on my left. The engine burst into life, I checked the oil pressure, and looked up to clear the right engine. Before I could start it, I was startled by the sight of our Twin Beech 18 rolling backwards through the field across the runway, at high speed, it took my breath away. There was no use starting the right engine now. It looked as though there would be damage after a ground loop like that and it would be extensive. I pulled the mixture, stopped the left engine and looked at the instructor, I said, "Well, guess I won't need the multi-engine rating after all." He opened the door and we headed toward old 28Z.

While we trotted across the field, the engines were still ticking over. Gracie finally shut them down and the propellers chugged to a stop. Even from here I couldn't make out what was damaged but it didn't matter. On our budget, even a minor repair would be tough to pay for. This would certainly put an end to our dreams of flying a Twin Beech this summer.

As we neared the airplane, Gracie and her daughter stepped out of the rear door and stood there hugging each other, both were shaken but suffered no injury.

"What happened Gracie?" I asked. She didn't really know. Right after touchdown, the Beech switched ends and left the right side of the runway. It had gone through a 15-foot ditch and up the other side and rolled to a stop, BACKWARDS.

I started looking around 28Z for damage. Walking around the right side I heard Gracie yell at me to come over and look. She was pointing to the left landing gear and said, "There's something wrong with this brake Mike. Let me know when you get it fixed and I'll be out to fly again." She and her daughter simply turned away and walked back across the runway satisfied that the incident was no fault of hers.

There was nothing wrong with that brake, the disk is supposed to float freely inside the brake housing and that's what Gracie indicated was the cause of the ground loop. The real good news was, there was also nothing wrong with 28Z. Gracie had lost control on landing, rolled at least 3,000 feet, in reverse, initially at high speed, through the ditch, across the field, and left not a SCRATCH anywhere on the airplane. I was elated; we would still have a Twin Beech for the summer! My two partners showed up with a tug and tow bar and as they hooked up the airplane, they sent me back to the Twin Comanche to finish my lesson.

Gracie never flew the Beech again even though she begged me to do so. The week before, I had ignored warnings from several of the experienced pilots on Columbine Airport advising me not to let her fly the airplane. I reasoned she had flown everything from B-17s to P-47s as a WASP during the war. Unfortunately, time had eroded her abilities despite the fact that she had continued flying over the years. I had my multi rating the following Tuesday.

The Beech was a ball to fly. I loved learning her secrets every weekend. Columbine was a little tight for a Beech 18. When we loaded up the jumpers and taxied down the narrow 1,000 ft. taxiway to runway 30, wing walkers would clear each wing tip so I didn't clip one of the tied down airplanes. The runway was narrow but manageable and the 4,000 foot length was just enough for a fully grossed Beech 18 taking off at 5,700 feet above sea level on a hot summer day. For a couple of weeks jumpers would show up on weekdays to jump the new airplane. After dark, we would finish packing the parachutes and walk over to the Beech with a cooler full of beer and sit inside or outside on the wing and admire our treasure.

I had just gotten my commercial ticket a month earlier because the local FAA inspector who showed up one weekend didn't agree that we were a parachute club. It was true, we were a commercial drop zone and we should have had commercial licenses and he busted one of our pilots. Luckily, I was jumping when he showed up or it would have been me.

The first weekend I began to fly jumpers in the Beech I was pulling the props through, and guess who showed up again; the same inspector who had busted our pilot. Today he was all smiles and congratulated me on passing my commercial exam. I guess he had been keeping an eye out for it. He then admired the Beech and asked who was going to be our pilot. When I told him I was, he looked at his partner in surprise and asked me when I had gotten a multi-rating.

"Last Tuesday," I told him. Then he asked how much time I had in the Beech,

"Two hours," I said. He and his friend just looked at each other and walked away shaking their heads, much to my relief.

By September I had 54 hours in the old girl and I was starting to get comfortable with her. We had several storms and wind gusts blow through on some of the days I was flying, but found the Beech more stable on landing in a crosswind than the skittish Cessna 180s. Only once did I have to divert to Arapahoe County Airport (now called Centennial Airport).

One evening my partners asked me not to have a drink because they wanted to go for a joy ride. I complied with their request and we tore up the skies over town that evening. Denver wasn't all that big in 1972 and we attracted the attention of the police helicopter for some reason. I was keeping an eye out for him anyway and when he started following us back to the airport I implemented plan B. I knew I could outrun him but we wouldn't be able to get off the airport before he caught up so I flew towards Arapahoe County Airport instead of Columbine. Arapahoe didn't have a tower and the Beech didn't have a transponder in those days. As soon as I was over the airport, I turned off the lights and banked steeply toward Columbine. My partners all yelled in delight when I made one more steep turn, but when I told them about the police helicopter they began to sober up.

I was a little surprised at how much I had to concentrate landing this thing on a pitch black night. The runway lights at Columbine made the narrow 4,000 foot runway look a lot shorter and narrower than it was and the old Beech seemed to be going a lot faster too. I waited until short final to turn on the landing lights (Arapahoe Airport was behind us to the east) and lit the navigation lights as well. I made a picture perfect landing and we rolled out to the end of the runway (over the years I have learned that you make your best landings when you're scared to death). I turned the landing lights out again as we turned around and taxied toward our tie-down keeping an eye out for the helicopter. There was no sign of him following us. We left the Beech in her spot and jumped into our cars and I could now join in with the party.

September is often the best weather of the year in Colorado and we were taking advantage of it before the cold winter months would bring our business to a near standstill. We were making plans to fly the Beech out west for a couple of weekends just to keep her busy and we could always gather up enough skydivers to pay for the fuel it took to fly out and back.

On the morning of November 17, I loaded up the Volkswagen bus with bags, parachutes, skydivers, and girlfriends, then headed for Columbine just before sunrise. We had been invited to fly the Beech to Elsinore, California for their 10-man star competition. I had really been looking forward to the long cross-country flight. I'd only done this long a flight once before in the 180, but as the dawn began to break I could see the mountains to the west were shrouded in clouds. The roads were covered with snow and ice from the overnight storms.

A brand new Beech 18 pilot!

It was cold that morning, but we Coloradans were accustomed to it. We loaded the Beech and closed the door as I climbed into the left seat. I primed the heck out of the old 985 Pratt & Whitney then hit the starter button. The propeller barely moved at first but gained momentum as the oil loosened up inside the engine and the battery warmed a little. Still, there was no sign of life from that old Pratt so I started using up every cold start trick I knew. It was to no avail, there was not even a cough from any of the cylinders. Then the battery began to give up, I sat there cursing. Denny Button, a skydiver and A&P mechanic came up and said he would try to prop start the engine and asked me to keep priming it like I had been.

Denny and several of the jumpers got out of the airplane and walked to the front of the left engine. They stomped down the snow as solidly as they could and Denny started propping the engine. I didn't give us a chance in heck that we could start the 985 this way but it was our last option. He pulled on the prop for several minutes until he just ran out of steam and stepped back to take a break. I asked if he was okay and he smiled and said to just give him a minute and he'd try some more. Finally Denny stepped back up to the engine. The blades had stopped in a vertical position so he reached for the bottom blade and laid his gloved hand on the face. He stopped to look up at me and asked if I was ready, was everything on. I could see he was still tired but he wanted to leave as badly as I did so I told him everything was ready. Denny pulled the lower blade a few inches so that he could reach the top blade then reach up and moved it a couple of inches lower to get a better grip. That's when it happened. Instead of stopping in a position where Denny could reach the blade easily, it kept going. It was a slow movement at first, there was no sound from the engine but the blades started rotating, slowly at first, gradually picking up speed. Denny's eyes were as wide as saucers when he realized what was happening. He rotated his left shoulder forward and stepped back from the airplane as the engine came to life. Denny looked up at me with a big smile and saluted. I could read his lips saying, "See, I told you I could do it!" He was a lucky man.

Everyone loaded back inside while I started the right engine and waited for both to warm up before taxiing out to the runway.

I figured I was going to have to fly south to get around this storm. After takeoff we leveled off below the higher mountain peaks because of the low clouds, crossed over Kenosha Pass and flew down Highway 285 through South Park looking for a way through. I could see over Trout Creek Pass and flew past Buena Vista heading south again. Poncha Pass was closed in solid and Monarch Pass was even worse to the west. I turned around and decided to take a look up around Leadville.

It was cold in that old Twin Beech despite using full heat. The windshield kept icing over on the inside. The girlfriends were the only ones with credit cards and we used them to scrape the ice off. As we passed Buena Vista, northbound this time, I noticed the clouds had lifted a little so I started to climb again, at 12,000 feet I could see the other side of Cottonwood Pass, it was open. I climbed until we were just below the cloud base and cleared Cottonwood at 14,000 feet. We had oxygen but no masks. We would hand a plastic tube around any time someone felt they needed a hit.

The weather was overcast passing Gunnison, but we had plenty of ceiling and good visibility so I pressed on but it still looked like I wasn't going to be able to go south. Over Montrose I could see the San Juan Mountains were closed solid so I headed towards Grand Junction to get some fuel. We had been flying for two hours and covered only 169 miles from Columbine Airport.

In Grand Junction, I checked weather to Las Vegas. The weather in Las Vegas was fine, but en-route was nasty. The briefer said the tops were reported at 11000 feet so I figured I could make the 2 hour flight on top if I needed. I filled both main tanks and headed west again, feeling a lot better about our chances of making it to the west coast. We would land in Las Vegas just before sunset and get a hotel then leave early tomorrow morning for Elsinore.

I followed Interstate 70 as long as I could but by Green River we were on top of the overcast. About an hour out I had to climb up to 12,000 feet then 14,000 to stay above the clouds and the visibility behind us was deteriorating. I wasn't able to pick up any of the navigation fixes on the radio along the midpoint of my route so I tuned in a couple behind me to try to get a ground speed. I tuned Hanksville on 115.9 hoping to find out how far west we were. The OBS needle swung to the left and there was a TO indication. I dawned on me that we hadn't passed it yet. That meant our ground speed at 14,000 feet was only about half of what I expected. Sure enough, by my calculation we were only going 85 mph which meant almost 100 mph of headwind. I turned slightly south to check behind me and the clouds were closing in, going back to Junction was not going to be possible without having to fly through icy clouds, in the dark!

I started going over my options. Everything below was socked in and I didn't have the experience to try a low instrument approach in the mountains. I was still three hours from Las Vegas at my present speed and only a little over two hours fuel remaining in the tank. On top of that, there was only an hour of daylight left. I looked at my passengers and friends still partying in the back and I couldn't believe I had put them in this position. The only thing I could do was carry on toward Las Vegas and hope we would break through the overcast high enough to be able to see the ground when the engines ran out of gas.

It seemed like an hour but 20 minutes passed and I decided it was time to break the news to someone besides myself. I looked around at the solid overcast below us, it was obscuring everything and the clouds were starting to turn pink because of the setting sun. I was scared. I called Denny to the front, he was a student pilot but I thought a second opinion might be useful. As he was crawling over the drunk skydivers toward the cockpit I scanned the horizon hoping to see a break in the endless cloud layer ahead. Denny sat down in the right seat and smiled but when he saw the look on my face he asked what was wrong. I told him what our ground speed was and he did a mental calculation then said, "So we'll be in Las Vegas after dark, right?" I looked ahead one more time trying to think how to tell Denny we had only an hour and a half worth of gas and that wasn't going to get us to Las Vegas when something caught my eye below and to the left.

WOW! There was a runway. It wasn't much of an opening in the overcast but it was just big enough to circle down through. I handed Denny the map and rolled into a steep left spiral. I was determined to keep that runway in sight. Denny dialed in the unicom frequency and identified the airport as Bryce Canyon. The runway was very narrow, but plenty long. I called on the radio and told them I was overhead and I was going to land. A lady called back and advised we couldn't land yet because they had just started plowing the runway. That's why that black strip of blacktop looked so narrow. They had made only one pass with the snowplow.

I had my eyes glued to that black strip and I advised the lady on the unicom that it didn't matter what shape the runway was, "We're landing!" I dropped the gear and flaps, lined up on final and made another one of those perfect landings (remember scared to death). As we taxied in I began to shake with relief, Denny said, "Damn Larson, it doesn't seem that cold here why are you shaking so much?" That's when I spilled the beans and let him know how much trouble we were in and why I asked him to come forward. He shook his head smiling, "Ah Larson, I knew you'd get us through." He hadn't quite thought things through yet.

I pulled up to the fuel pump and we crawled out of the airplane and I was still shaking. None of the skydivers knew why, they just thought I was cold. I looked up at the sky and it was overcast again. Our life saving break was gone. We topped the tanks and the attendant told us we could stay in the airport office for the night because there were no motels around. I called flight service to check the weather and Las Vegas was still good. We were seeing breaks in the overcast going by regularly now so we decided to take-off.. I climbed through the breaks and the sun was just setting. Within a few minutes I could see the lights of Cedar City ahead then St. George and finally the lights of Las Vegas. The wind had calmed down a bit but it still took two more hours to reach LAS. I was too mad at myself to party with my friends. Exhausted from the experience I slept soundly.

The next morning the flight to Elsinore was routine compared to the day before. I was ashamed of getting myself and all of my friends in that predicament and vowed I would never allow it to happen again, and I haven't. We were at the drop zone in time to use the airplane for the meet and I flew four and one half hours each day. That was enough to make it a profitable trip and I was very happy, aside from the first day, about how this was turning out.

Over the weekend we met with a couple of Arizona jumpers, Jerry and John Willsey. I inquired about taking the Beech to their drop zone this winter and they said YEA!! NEXT WEEKEND!! They were organizing a twenty-man star attempt and so far had not engaged the second airplane. They had an AT-11 (military version of the Twin Beech 18) on their drop zone and thought they would use three or four Cessnas to get everyone in the air at the same time but they preferred another Beech. I talked to my passengers about flying to Phoenix and hanging out until next weekend and all of the jumpers eagerly agreed but, the girls had jobs and it had been a stretch for them to get Monday off for this trip. They had paid their fair share of the expenses so I felt obligated to get them home on time.

Monday morning we loaded up in 28Z and headed to Denver. I planned another fuel stop in Las Vegas so I could check the weather again. We had a late breakfast there and I could already see the clouds building over the mountains to the east of Las Vegas. The weather briefer described exactly the same conditions I had gotten in trouble with on the first day. There was no way I was going to let that happen again and that was all the excuse we needed, we headed for Phoenix.

Jerry had told us he lived near Falcon Field east of Tempe so we landed there and gave him a call. He was excited that we had decided to fly in. He jumped in his pickup and hauled all of us and our gear to his house. The girls got on the phone and begged for a week off from their jobs but each one had to make a reservation on Frontier Airlines to go home that afternoon. None could stay the whole week and still have a job when they got back.

I mean to tell you, these Arizona people knew how to party. We were having the time of our life. I had to stay sober one night while they made a night jump into Jerry's house, but I held my own every other day. The week went by pretty quickly while we basked in the warm Arizona sun. Saturday morning I flew down to the drop zone at "Casa Grande." I flew the Beech over 18 hours that week and I was rolling in the money. When I got back to Columbine and made the deposit we would be well positioned to make it through the winter in Colorado. .

The weather had finally cleared up over the mountains for the flight home. I stopped in Durango for fuel and then on to Columbine. It only took four and one half hours to get back. I'll never forget arriving over the foothills in smooth air, the Beech descending just below the red line as I crossed overhead of Columbine Airport and made a long 270 turn to the left and entered downwind at gear speed. I felt like the conquering hero returning from battle and ready to receive my accolades on arrival. The near disastrous first day was still in the back of my mind, but I had successfully completed the trip without breaking anything and I had a load of cash stashed in my back pocket for the effort. When I showed my partners how much the deposit was, they treated me like a hero, especially when I told them we had been invited back to Casa Grande anytime to fly more jumpers.

If you are reading this and you're not a skydiver you probably don't know how Casa Grande, Arizona, became a significant footnote in parachuting history. We made several flights back there and the jumpers kept begging us to return. The guys running the parachute center weren't as enthusiastic about sharing the weekend revenue. They finally advised me not to come back unless we were invited by them. Unfortunately for them, however, we had just bought the Casa Grande FBO. Columbine had been sold by the sleazy owner and the airport would soon be sprouting houses. We were moving the whole operation to Arizona. The Arizona operators didn't like being second fiddle on the airport so they packed up and moved their operation to Coolidge. Most of the experienced skydivers stayed with us at Casa Grande and by February we were busier in Arizona in the winter than we were in Colorado in the summer.

I enjoy the occasional opportunity to revisit flying a Beech 18 again and wish they weren't so expensive to operate or I'd have another one of my own. Someday, I am going to fly our Cessna 195 back to Bryce Canyon Airport and give thanks for saving my bacon on that cold November day in 1972.

3

HOW TO MAKE A LIVING IN AVIATION

In 1973, in Casa Grande, Arizona, we were operating a Lockheed Lodestar and two Beech 18s for the experienced jumpers, but we needed a single-engine Cessna for training students. In this business, the income from the experienced jumpers barely paid for gas and maintenance. We couldn't afford insurance so we didn't have any. Money made in skydiving was from training new students at $65.00 for their first jump. We would canvas Arizona State University and U of A every couple of weeks and usually train 25 or 30 new jumpers a weekend. We were training them to jump from the Twin Beech, but that was expensive and less than ideal.

I knew of a Cessna 195 for sale in Eloy, Arizona, about 20 miles from our drop zone in Casa Grande. The airplane had been for sale for more than a year and I thought it could be had for less than $4,000.00. That was a lot of money in the 70s but we managed to save most of it in a few weeks and I caught a ride over to Eloy to make the offer. After only a few minutes, we settled on a price of $3,400, and I pulled the cash out of my pocket and handed it to the broker.

I'll never forget Bob Haskins throwing me he keys to N3451V and telling me how much I was going to like this airplane. It didn't start out that way! I had been flying C-180s and always prided myself in being able to start the Continental 0-470 engine hot or cold. The key was knowing how much fuel you wanted to give her by pumping the throttle just the right number of times. The same goes for the 985 Pratts on the Twin Beech so why should a 195 be any different?

I climbed in between the two front seats, made myself comfortable, noted how bad the visibility was to the right of the nose and switched on the master switch. I pushed in the mixture and as soon as I could find the starter button I yelled, "Clear Prop." I knew enough to let the prop turn several blades before turning on the mags (I didn't even know it didn't have two of them) so I took the opportunity to pump the throttle a couple of times to prime the engine. I quickly turned the ignition switch to both, but the engine didn't even cough. Maybe, I thought, it needed a couple more pumps of the throttle.

That's when I heard that awful sound, "Kawumpf!" It was a terrible sound. It sounded like a muffled explosion and that's just what it was. I had caught radial engines on fire before and I knew all I needed to do was keep turning the engine until it started and that would blow out the fire, but this engine wasn't showing any signs of starting. Worse yet, the battery was beginning to give up and I had no idea if there was a fire extinguisher to be found in all of Eloy, Arizona. Just as I was thinking I needed to bail out of this thing and watch it burn to the ground, Bob rushed in and sprayed CO_2 into the cowling and the fire was out.

I looked at Bob stupidly through the open window and he shook his head and said, "By the way Mike, I forgot to tell you, use the primer to start the engine, and... whatever you do... don't pump the throttle or it'll catch fire."

I thought, *Good advice Bob, Thanks for having a fire extinguisher handy.* Then he told me I should initially start the engine on battery then switch to both after it fired. OK, easy enough. I primed it two strokes, yelled "Clear" and after a few blades I turned the switch to battery. The old jake fired right up.

I had heard the term "Shaky Jake" before so I wasn't concerned with the way she idled as I taxied to the end of the runway. Taxiing actually seemed easier than the Beech but only slightly trickier than the 180. Not being able to see over the right side of the nose was uncomfortable at first but a few S-turns quickly returned my confidence that the 195 and I could get along. I soon found out that we would indeed be able to get along. Once I brought the power up on takeoff and 51V started revealing her secrets to me, my love affair with the 195 began to blossom. Only a Jake or Continental radial can create this unique sensation. The vibration, the torque, the acceleration, even the visual sensation as you bring the throttle slowly up to full power will grab all of your senses and tell you to hold on tight, this is going to be one heck of a ride.

We flew 51V more than three years and could always rely on her to climb with four or five jumpers, descend empty all weekend long and then fly us home every night. Once in a while we'd give her some fresh oil but that was about all she required between annual inspections. The 195 is the most reliable airplane I have ever owned.

One week we had to go to Los Angeles for a day and then fly up to San Francisco to see about a business opportunity. We spent the first night in Los Angeles and then headed north to San Francisco along the coast at 500 ft. The weather was gorgeous all the way until we ran into fog just south of SFO. I tried circling around until I could find a way across the bridge but we barely had a brief glimpse of the Golden Gate and decided to turn around. You couldn't do this today with the bay area traffic, but it was still legal then. We circled south of SJC and tried to go north across Oakland, but the fog was not going to let us through.

Cessna 195 full of jumpers at Casa Grande, Arizona.

We landed at Alameda and found a place for lunch and checked weather. It wasn't going to cooperate so we called off our business and decided to head back to Arizona. The first leg got us to Palm Springs just after sunset and I wasn't looking forward to the night flight through the desert to Phoenix, but my passengers insisted that we press on since we didn't have the money for a motel. In fact, as we counted out how much money we had between the three of us, there was only $20.00 for gas and that would barely buy enough to reach Glendale just west of Phoenix.

Once again I made the case to stay the night rather than try a minimum fuel night desert crossing. I won't say I was overruled; let's just say there was a convincing reason for us to get back that night.

If we weren't at the parachute center the next morning to fly the weekend business, we might not have much to eat that next week. The gas truck showed up and I told the line boy how much money we had but that we could really use an extra five gallons to get across the vast stretch of the Sonora Desert. He wasn't impressed, he said something like, "This ain't no charitable organization!" Well, that was the last card I had to play so I gathered up all of our cash and headed to the FBO to check weather and my fuel calculation. When I paid the bill it was right to the penny and I walked out of there with nothing in my pockets except a pilot's license and I wasn't too happy to have that at the moment. I had refigured the distance and harbored even less confidence about our range, we decided if it started looking too close we would drop into Buckeye, Arizona, and borrow a couple gallons from them when they opened in the morning. I crawled into old 51V with an ominous feeling about this flight and I hate to start out like that but we strapped in anyway.

I turned on the master and started to prime the engine and checked the fuel gauges. Darn, the line boy didn't give us that extra five gallons I had begged for; in fact, we found there was at least 10 gallons more fuel than we had paid for. We all broke into smiles of relief and looked around for the line boy, to at least say thanks, but he was nowhere in sight. It was a beautiful night desert crossing after all and my faith in mankind was given another boost that magical evening.

Many of you know it's not easy to keep food on the table and work in general aviation. The early 70s were good times for small airplanes. The factories were manufacturing record numbers of new airplanes and having very little problems selling them. The used market was good for airplanes with Continental and Lycoming engines, but radial engines were out of favor with the general public, which made it possible for guys like us to afford our Beech 18s, Lockheed Lodestar, and Cessna 195. We bought the Lodestar for about $5,000.00. Sure it was expensive to run but gas was only 35 or 40 cents a gallon so it was pretty much a break-even airplane for us. Not the 195 though. That old work horse actually kept making money every week. Granted, we weren't buying insurance and we were doing all of our own maintenance, but 51V never failed to pay her own way.

Author and his business partner Bob Schaffer. Bob is smiling now until he found out he would be working on the Lodestar by himself that day.

I think it was a Wednesday morning when three guys showed up asking about filming in the desert. These guys smelled of Hollywood; they all wore expensive clothes and sunglasses and you could sure tell who the boss was and who was a lackey. Two of the guys were so attentive to the boss's needs it made you sick. Being a so-called entrepreneur and my own boss, I thanked my lucky stars that I didn't have to do that myself. Turns out these guys were indeed from Hollywood and they needed a desert landscape to film a commercial and they wanted to charter a plane to scout around in. The dollar signs flashed in my eyes as I told them I was their man if they could just give us an hour to reinstall the seats and door on that old reliable Cessna 195. They agreed to wait and actually agreed to the hourly charge of $50.00 for the plane and pilot. I looked at my smiling partner, Bob

Schaffer, and gave him the thumbs up and we both knew we were going to eat well tonight. Bob kept smiling until he realized he would be doing all the wrenching on the Lodestar for the next couple of hours. Somebody had to be schmoozing with the Hollywood types up in the 195. When you have partners in the airplane business, it's good to be the pilot, it gives you more flexibility.

We had the plane ready when our marks came back from lunch and we loaded up. I was going to be the best desert guide that you ever met. Immediately, I headed north to a secluded area not far from the airport. It wasn't really what they described to me what they were looking for, but I didn't want them to find the perfect place for at least an hour so I could get my 50 bucks. No problem, our talented film maker informed me and his two hangers-on that he thought the best location would be north of Scottsdale and we should head up there. My grin started to exceed the breaking point, Scottsdale and back would be at least an hour and a half, wow, 75 bucks.

We started scouting around the area but nothing was quite right. The hour turned into two hours and still they hadn't found the right place. We would circle an area and the three marks would yell back and forth about the attributes of the landscape's "personality" and how it would look when framed properly and which filter would be required for the camera. No kidding, all three of them would look out the window and actually frame the area with their thumbs and forefingers to form a square simulating the camera frame. In the meantime, I'm watching the tach time steadily rolling over and using my thumb and forefingers practicing my multiplication tables.

Let's see, $50.00 X 1.8 is... I found myself hanging on every word boss was saying and if he said, "Go North boy," I said, "Yessir, I can go north!" I was willing to comply with any request because he had the money, for now. I was now certainly more sympathetic with my two fellow lackeys.

After a couple of hours the boss wanted to take a break, so we dropped into Scottsdale for a snack and to ask the locals about the ideal location in the desert. I taxied up to the FBO and kept a wary eye out for a certain FAA inspector that was an acquaintance of mine and might be at work in the FSDO office next door. I herded everyone inside as inconspicuously as I could. Boss went to the restroom and one of the lackeys couldn't wait to tell me about him. It turned out that boss was the guy who coined the slogan, "You'll wonder where the yellow went when you brush your teeth with *Pepsodent*." I was duly impressed. I had grown up listening to that on television. He had made a bundle on that advertising campaign and this was going to be his next big commercial. That's why they were so particular about the location. They were going to do a commercial for *Ray-O-Vac* batteries and the desolate location would emphasize the reliability of their batteries.

I, of course, understood immediately the importance of our business now, all I could hear was a cash register going "Kaching." After another hour and a half in the 195, we headed back to Casa Grande, bitterly disappointed (not) that we had failed to find our perfect location for the commercial. On the ground, I could hardly believe my eyes as the boss started peeling off those beautiful one hundred dollar bills. He gave me two of them. I looked at Bob grinning from ear-to-ear through his grease covered face and we both headed for the best steak in Casa Grande. We knew we could afford a good dinner because Mr. "you wonder where the yellow went" made us promise to be ready for another flight bright and early tomorrow at 11 a.m. Yes sir. We were in the money.

I am sad to say we had another tough day finding that perfect location. I flew to Cave Creek, Gila Bend, Picacho Peak, and even to Oracle. No place was good enough for the boss's comeback commercial. Again it started to get late and I could see the stress building as the marks confided to me that a whole film crew and actors would be heading for their site Saturday morning and they still hadn't found it yet.

This is what it must have looked like as we flew over the Sonora Desert looking for the perfect spot to film a commercial.

It was time to head back to Casa Grande while they discussed what they were going to do, all the time they looked desperately at the passing landscape. I started to slow the 195 as we neared the airport and climbed to pattern altitude. On downwind, while I was concentrating on where the runway might be, I heard a loud exclamation, "LOOK!" from the right seat. All three passengers became instantly excited and asked me to turn the plane around and take them back where we had just passed. I did a grand 360 and watched in amazement as all three filmmakers congratulated each other because they had finally found the perfect location to film their *Ray-O-Vac* commercial. Right there below us, not 1,000 feet north of the runway of the Casa Grande Airport was their spot. After landing they borrowed my old F-150 pickup truck and rushed to the site. Bob and I started pulling the seats out and the door off the 195, since a few hard core jumpers always showed up on Friday. Our heroes returned from the desert still excited about their success and again Bob and I grinned while two more beautiful one hundred dollar bills found their way into our pockets. *Man, steak! Two nights in a row!*

The next hurdle was to get permission from the city manager to film on the airport, and I was asked to make those arrangements. I agreed to talk to the bureaucrats on their behalf. Notice I didn't say I would get permission. My relations with the city manager were less than cordial. In fact, I wasn't even sure he would let me in his office, but I felt obligated to try because of those hundred dollar bills in my pocket. There wasn't much else that could get me to do it. And I did try, but the butthead wouldn't even consider it. Perhaps it was due to our past dealing that he didn't believe my story about the famous Hollywood producer wanting to shoot a movie at the Casa Grande Airport, he sent me packing. I know he was hoping the parachute center would be out of business soon and get off of his precious airport. Fat chance though, I still had two hundred bucks in my pocket.

I called Hollywood and told them the bad news, and reminded them we could put the seats back in the 195 if they needed, but boss graciously declined and said he would call the studio and make the arrangements. I don't know what they did, but early Saturday morning the cameras, actors, horses plus a helicopter all showed up and they filmed that commercial all day. About four months later I saw the commercial on TV and I was disappointed that there were no credits for the flight crew. Actually, they don't do credits on commercials.

I got to thinking about this experience. The passenger business wasn't all that bad. Maybe I ought to get an instrument rating and do some charter flying. Heck, if it weren't for the fact that I had to wear these darn glasses, maybe even an airline job.

The last couple of days beat the crap out of sitting on top of that old Lodestar with a hammer (or monkey wrench) trying to keep it flying for another couple days. Corporate might be an option, but then I'd have to kiss up to some boss like I saw (did) this week. No, I can't afford, nor do I need an instrument ticket to fly skydivers. And how could I keep flying these old round engine birds if I had to go to work flying for someone else. Not a chance.

4

LOOKING FOR A LITTLE HELP

Man, sometimes I used to fly so much at the parachute center that I would be desperate to find and check out a new pilot. It seems like I would fly for six-months straight before some new guy would show up and I would get a six month break from flying and jump on the weekends instead. It was late September and I had been through one of the flying stages and I was really getting tired of hauling the Cessna 195 and Beech 18 up to altitude and race the jumpers down to do it all over again. The busy season was just about to arrive for us and I knew I had to find a pilot soon. Eloy, Arizona was about 20 miles southeast of Casa Grande and I remembered that the guy who ran the spray operation there had a son who was just breaking in as a spray pilot and their season was about to slow down. I figured that boy was going to look for some flying during the winter. He had a multi rating and a lot of tail dragger time so he would be perfect for the 195 and then we could check him out in the Beech.

I wandered over to Eloy during the week in the 195 to see if I could talk to him but I knew that I would first have to convince the old man that his son would be safe. The 195 was as clean as I could get her, for a jump plane. I knew the old man was going to look her over carefully. I gave him my best sales pitch about how safe we tried to operate and I would keep the kid away from the skydivers when he was not flying so he would not be tempted to start jumping and partying with our more rambunctious types on the drop zone. He wasn't much impressed and especially didn't

Our trusty old Twin Beech climbing over Casa Grande, Arizona with a rowdy load of skydivers. Note the peace sign taped on the nose of the aircraft.

want the boy around our hell-raising crowd but knew the kid wanted to fly and could use a little experience before the cotton season started the next summer. Surprisingly, he agreed to come over the next weekend and take a look at our operation. That wasn't exactly what I wanted to hear but I didn't have much choice. We had a group of jumpers coming over from Southern California and some from Salt Lake City and it promised to be a busy weekend. If I could keep the old crop duster and his son occupied, they might not get too cozy with the jumpers and maybe I would still get my pilot for the winter.

Author impatiently waiting for the weather to clear so we could start another weekend of flying.

The weather on Saturday turned out to be nasty for the Sonora Desert. The wind was blowing and the overcast was down to about a thousand feet. The forecast was for improving ceilings in the afternoon so everyone was sitting around waiting for a break in the weather. Everyone except: Ed Dugan. dEd (as he was nicknamed) was an F-100 instructor pilot out of Tucson and he commuted up to Casa Grande every Friday or Saturday in his trusty old Cessna 170 to jump with us. dEd, like most fighter pilots, was easily bored so, instead of sitting around, he proceeded to treat everyone to a low level aerobatic performance in his commuter plane. It was a masterful performance, I stood outside the hangar and watched him roll and loop and hammerhead up into and back out of the clouds. dEd was doing things in the 170 that you wouldn't think possible. He had the right door off in case we needed the extra lift that weekend, but he was the only one in the plane. Just as dEd disappeared into the overcast in a vertical climb during a loop, I felt more than saw two people walk up and stand beside me watching the demonstration. The 170 reappeared out of the overcast, still vertical, but this time in the opposite direction. IT WAS AWESOME!

I looked down for a moment to see who might be standing beside me and there he was, my new pilot, grinning from ear to ear, enjoying the heck out of the show. Problem was, sonny's Dad was also standing there and he was not grinning. I wasn't too worried, as soon as I explained that dEd was an experienced combat fighter pilot just back from the Vietnam and a man with that kind of experience knew exactly what he was doing. He would have to agree it was perfectly safe. For a nanosecond, the old man's frown moderated somewhat, but then he looked me in the eye and told me in no uncertain terms that he had to follow the rules in his business and, "That there fighter pilot should damn well know better than anyone that he should not be doing that in a Cessna 170 and at that altitude."

I'm thinking, some people just don't get it and, this might be a little harder sale than I first thought. I saw that dEd was leveling out from the loop and he throttled back like he was done and would land. I was hoping that the last loop was the only part of the show the old crop duster and his boy had seen. I decided to change tack a little and I told the old man he was right. I would have to talk to dEd about what he had done and ask him not to do it again. In the mean time, dEd was circling around to the south, obviously lining up for a buzz job through the drop zone full of cheering skydivers. dEd leveled off at about 25 feet and I was relieved that this would be a conservative buzz job, not the usual "two feet off the sage brush" with skydivers diving for the sand to save their butts from getting ground up in the prop. Just as I was about to begin my final sales pitch to my new pilot's father, a loud roar of applause and approval rose from the delighted crowd of observers. I looked up at dEd, but no one was in the pilot's seat! I couldn't help but double over laughing and guffawing loudly as I saw the 170 go by. dEd was standing sideways where the right seat would have been. His left hand was wrapped around the seatbelt, flying with his right hand and, his head turned to the right so he could watch where he was going. It was quite a feat of airmanship, especially when as he flew past us, I could see his pants peeled down to his ankles and his bare ass hanging out the open door. It is a moon that I will never forget or probably ever see again, I couldn't stop laughing and I had to hold onto the hangar to keep from falling on the ramp and rolling over and over. The things you get to see in this crowd just CRACK ME UP!

A moon I'll probably never see again.

Oh dear!! I remembered all of a sudden, my new pilot and his old man saw the same thing. I wondered if the old fart would crack a smile after seeing that! Unfortunately, I will never know the answer, but I can guess. When I looked around to check on them they were nowhere to be found. I saw a large dust cloud rising from an old pickup truck exiting the airport as fast as it would go heading, I assumed, back to Eloy and the safety of home.

As the overcast began to break up I headed over to the old Beech and began pulling the props through and checking her out, all the time cursing that damn Dugan. I ought to make him fly jumpers all damn weekend, but there he is, his usual handsome smile and his parachute strapped on, waiting for me to crawl into the left seat. I was going to have to look elsewhere for my new pilot.

Ed Dugan relaxes after a hard day of flying and skydiving at Casa Grande.

5

THE LODESTAR BLUES

During the 1970s, we were running the FBO at Casa Grande Airport south of Phoenix, Arizona. We had a Cessna 195, Beech C-18 and D-18 and an old Lockheed Lodestar L-18 and relied on the jumpers for income. They would drive or fly from Phoenix and Tucson every weekend and most would stay the night in their vans or campers, some in tents and a few would sleep in the airplanes. There were lively parties every weekend and that was part of the enjoyment of our endeavor. The parties lasted all winter until the Sonora Desert started to return to its famously hot temperatures in late April and we found the skydiving activities would start to taper off, much as they would during the winter months in the north.

The first year we had the Lodestar it did quite well for us but there were a few close calls learning how to operate properly that old girl. A Lodestar is built for speed, the rigors of climbing to 12 or 14 thousand feet and slowing to near stall speed on jump run presented challenges that a bunch of 20-year olds didn't, at first, understand and had to overcome, sometimes the hard way. We did survive a successful winter and looked for a way to keep the airplane busy through the miserable Arizona summer. The obvious answer was to take the airplane north and several of the jumpers from the Seattle area assured us we would keep it busy through early September. My partner, Bob Schaffer and I decided to send the plane there.

Our Lockheed Lodestar, Cessna 195 and one of the Beech 18s ready to get to work.

One of our pilots, Steve Gras, was anxious to continue flying the Lodestar and he volunteered to work the summer for us. Sometime in mid May, Steve and his girlfriend, Rita loaded up in the airplane and ferried to Renton Field south of Seattle. I loaded up my old six cylinder F150 pickup truck and started the long drive up with my girlfriend "Dobergator," a six month old Doberman puppy. As "Dobergator" and I headed down the final leg into Seattle, the sun was shining, wind calm and several parachutes dotted the sky while we drove into the Issaquah Drop Zone. I found Steve and Rita and we made plans for the next weekend with the Lodestar.

All of the Seattle jumpers were enthusiastic to have us there thru the summer and assured us they would keep the airplane full of jumpers. Issaquah was a quaint grass airstrip just north of Seattle and although the locals told us they had flown a Lodestar in and out of there, with jumpers, Steve and I decided the runway was too short to safely operate from and we notified everyone that we would be flying out of Arlington, a few miles further north. It took a few days to prepare the FBO in Arlington for the influx of activity on the weekends but they were cooperative and looked forward to the additional business. A local farmer made his fields available as the drop zone and we acquired an old school bus to ferry the jumpers back and forth to the airport. Steve and Rita and I appropriated some used telephone poles, lined them up in the packing area and screwed in some hooks for the jumpers to use to pack their parachutes. Friday afternoon we had everything ready for a busy and we hoped, a profitable weekend. The Lodestar was fueled with just enough gas to ferry to Arlington in the morning and fly two loads of jumpers.

We found the local skydivers partying that Friday evening and notified everyone all was ready and waiting for them in the morning. I left early and headed to Renton Airport to bed down in the airplane so we could fly to Arlington just after sunrise. After a couple of beers, I stretched out in the most level part of the cabin and Dobergator and I went to sleep. Sunrise seemed a little subdued when I awoke. Usually there were several early morning departures out of Renton but this morning it was unusually quiet. I sat up in my sleeping bag and opened the door to take a look. Dobergator jumped out to take care of her business and she disappeared in the fog only a few hundred feet from the airplane. This would mean a couple of hours delay before the fog burned off so I headed over to the café for breakfast. A couple of the local pilots were sitting in the booth next to me and they were commenting about how they had seen this kind of fog hang around for weeks at a time. That didn't sound encouraging but I dismissed the comment as just some pessimistic pilot who didn't really want to go flying in the first place. Along about noon however, I was getting a little concerned. The visibility had improved but only marginally and no one was attempting to depart Renton. I finally walked over to the FSS and heard the bad news. They didn't expect any VFR weather until Wednesday or Thursday and that was their most optimistic forecast. Once again I heard the story about the fog coming in one year and staying near the whole summer.

True to the forecast, the whole weekend was shot but we were not discouraged. Neither Steve nor I had ever seen fog last more than a couple of days and we couldn't believe we would be so unlucky as to be shut down by fog two weekends in a row. Unfortunately, we were wrong. Two weeks later we still hadn't seen the sun, the locals were sympathetic but they assumed we had heard of the famous and fickle Seattle weather when it comes to fog and we should have been prepared for this type of delay. They didn't realize how close to the margin a parachute center operated. We had a few more dollars between Steve and I but the money was not going to last much longer.

Friday evening it was still fogged in and the forecast was only slightly encouraging for the weekend. I was invited to meet the jumpers at the SeaTac Holiday Inn for the Friday night gathering but they had no idea how little money I had left. I walked into the Holiday Inn Bar with only $1.00 in my pocket, enough for one beer which I ordered and nursed for several hours. Again I left early and made my way to the Lodestar wondering what to do next. I was broke and homeless and if the fog didn't lift this weekend, I figured the dog and I would start hitchhiking back to Arizona. At least there I could make a little money flying jumpers in the 195 for the summer. It wasn't a good night's sleep. Finally, I dozed off around 4 a.m. but I was soon being disturbed by an unfamiliar sound. Some idiot was running up his airplane next to the Lodestar. My left eye felt like a flashlight was shining directly into it. I opened my eye just enough to be blinded by the sun! I was up in a flash, it was a crystal clear morning and I had been saved from sure starvation.

Finally, after three weeks, Saturday morning dawned bright and clear.

It took only a few moments to pre-flight the old bird and start her up and get takeoff clearance from the tower. When we landed at Arlington, a few early morning jumpers were ready to go, we loaded up and Steve took off with our first load. I was smiling broadly as I collected the money for the second load while the Lodestar droned overhead on jump run. Steve brought her down and didn't even have to shut down the engines while the second load boarded and they took off. I looked over at the packing area and the jumpers were smiling and repacking as fast as they could. This is why we brought the airplane up here, I thought, these guys are cooped up all winter here in Seattle and are ready to make some jumps as soon as the weather breaks. One of the jumpers walked over and handed me the money for the third load and I told him we would need to fuel the Lodestar before they could board. He acknowledged and returned to the jumpers to inform them what was happening.

In the meantime Steve had just dropped the second load and was steadily making his way back down. As he entered the pattern I was over at the fuel pump ready to get him back in the air as fast as possible. I could just make out a slight variation in the engine noise as Steve turned final but as he taxied up I could hear a distinct backfire coming from one of the engines. I'm thinking we might have to change a plug before the next load but when I saw the look on Steve's face I knew there was trouble. He told me about half way down, number one started vibrating and when he added power it would backfire loudly, something was not right and we needed to take the cowling off and find out what it was.

We got a few of the jumpers to help us push the plane to a spot where we could check out the engine and I refunded the money for the third load. A quick compression check revealed the number one cylinder pressure was low and Steve and I set to work and had it off before 1 PM. We had heard of a fellow at Boeing Field who stocked some Curtis Wright 1820 parts and we drove down to talk to him but he was closed for the weekend.

Monday morning we assaulted the Boeing Field operator with our tale of woe and he pulled out a brand new certified, yellow-tagged 1820 cylinder for only $200.00. I told him thanks but we just couldn't afford the bucks for that cylinder and asked if there might be something a little cheaper. I'll never forget the way this guy smiled at me. He knew we were in a bind and didn't have the money, he decided to take a chance and handed us that beautiful cylinder and asked that we pay him when we could. We made a beeline for the airplane and had the engine ready just before sunset. Steve started her up in a cloud of smoke and she ran beautifully, no backfiring, shaking, or wobbling was apparent. I smiled up at my pilot and made the sign for him to cut the engine and we'd get the cowling on and be ready for the next weekend. Steve pulled the mixture and as soon as the engine started coasting to a stop I could hear something squealing from inside the engine. To my dismay, the prop didn't just coast to a lazy stop, it slowed rapidly and the awful squealing became louder as the prop stopped abruptly. It was pretty obvious by then that the main bearing was shot and had frozen up. We weren't going to fly again until that engine had been replaced.

Steve and Rita and I went out for dinner that evening and I could see the questions in their eyes. What was I going to do next? I told them I had called Bob Schaffer, still in Arizona, and given him the bad news.

Schaffer was about to leave for Europe with a group of the most experienced jumpers in the country to demo the skydiving we had been doing in Casa Grande over the last year but he said he would run up to Falcon Field outside of Phoenix and talk to Arizona Air Power. They had several Lodestars sitting in the dirt with nowhere to go. Just maybe we could talk them out of one of those engines and get the same deal the gentleman at Boeing Field had offered. We all knew that was our last shot. If it didn't work we'd have to head back to Phoenix with our tails between our legs, leaving the Lodestar where she sat until next winter when the money would start rolling in again.

Next morning I got a phone call from Bob. The Falcon Field operators figured they had very little to lose and said they would loan us a firewall forward 1820 engine until next winter! I really couldn't believe it. I just hadn't expected that to work out after all of the other bad luck we had been having. Bob was leaving on his trip the next day so I would have to drive back down to Arizona and haul the engine back up to Seattle in my truck. I rushed over to Steve and Rita's to give them the good news and make plans for Steve to begin taking the engine off while I made a mad dash to Phoenix and back. I figured I had just enough money for gas and if we ate only once or twice a day, food. Steve's Karmann Ghia wasn't in the driveway when I arrived so I knocked on the door to ask their roommate where they had gone. She kind of demurred, but finally asked why I hadn't known they had left late last night. They had packed everything up and headed home to Chicago. Apparently, they'd had enough of the Lodestar Blues. I was a little disappointed but not really surprised. I would probably have done the same thing if I had been in their shoes and I really couldn't blame them.

Dobergator, my 6 month old Doberman never complained about our predicament.

Actually, now there was enough money to eat every day if I skipped a day here and there. My little girlfriend, Dobergator, never complained once. She happily jumped back in the pickup truck and we headed to the airplane to gather up our belongings and make the long trip back to Phoenix. We left by noon and headed south. I remember very little about that trip except that I was so tired by the time I got to Las Vegas, that I looked for a hitchhiker to help me drive. I found a likely long haired prospect and soon I was sound asleep while he drove toward Kingman. At sunrise he woke me up and told me he was too tired to drive any farther and wanted out in Kingman anyway. I drove the rest of the way into Tempe, Arizona and headed to a friend's house where I must have slept for two days trying to recover from my ordeal.

Finally I felt ready to drive over to Falcon Field and collect our "new" engine. The operator walked me out to one of the derelict Lodestars that had been sitting in his field for several years and pointed to the left engine. He figured it had been running pretty well when he had last flown the airplane and he would expect his money no later than October. With my fingers crossed behind my back, I assured him there would be no problem and asked if I could borrow a few tools to remove the engine. He showed me where the tools and fork lift were and looked at my old pickup truck and shook his head with disgust. He couldn't believe I was going to make it all the way back up to Seattle in that old piece of junk. Truth was, one of the rods in the old six cylinder was starting to make quite a bit of noise but I didn't have any other options (that old pickup ran for three more years with that rod screaming).

As I carefully began to disconnect the engine, I labeled every hose and wire and drew a picture of the fire wall to help me remember how to put it all back together again. I had never changed an engine before and I wanted to be as careful and thorough as I could. After a day or two, the engine was sitting in the back of the sagging pickup. The rear bumper was only a few inches from the pavement and I knew it would be a slow trip to Seattle. Dobergator and I headed north with the rod squealing every time I tried to push the engine too hard and the back end bouncing off the pavement every couple of miles when I didn't slow down enough for a dip in the road. We spent a night in Salt Lake City with some jumpers I knew and they fed us and gave us a bed and shower to recover from the long ride we had just been through, we weren't even half way! The next leg took another two days straight and I parked the pickup next to the Lodestar and crashed in the cabin for a long rest.

I spent the next few days gathering and borrowing tools to get started on the job. I was having trouble finding a fork lift to lower the propeller and engine, but finally I found a farmer who was interested in airplanes and sympathetic with my plight and he volunteered his equipment.

All it would cost would be a ride in the right seat while flying the jumpers. Off came the prop, then the engine and finally I could unload the pickup. I dropped the "new" engine right in front of the firewall. I went over my drawings and labeled the firewall fittings and made plans to lift the engine up and attach the motor mounts with the same bolts I had taken out a few days prior.

By the time everything was finished, it was late August. The weather had been beautiful the whole time and I fell in love with Seattle. There is quite a bit more to this engine change than I am willing to relate in this story but after weeks of trying everything I could think of, the job was finally done. Bob was back from Europe and came up to Seattle to help me with the final details and it was time to take the airplane back to Arizona. On the way, however, we would stop in Elsinore, California. It was hosting their annual Star Crest Scramble meet and asked that we provide the Lodestar to them that weekend to fly some of the hundreds of extra jumpers expected to attend over the Labor Day weekend.

About 10 or 12 Seattle skydivers wanted to go to Elsinore for the meet and they agreed to pay enough for us to cover the cost of fuel on the way down. We ferried back to Renton Field and Friday morning loaded everyone up and headed down to California. It was a beautiful flight. We stopped in Modesto, California for fuel and the Lodestar always attracted a lot of attention when we taxied up, usually from law enforcement. Most thought we were drug smugglers on our way to Mexico but when they saw the jumpers and parachutes laying all over the floor of the airplane they usually left us alone.

Changing the engine on the cantankerous old Lockheed Lodestar.

As we neared Elsinore I began to climb to 12,500 feet. The price the jumpers paid to go with us included a free jump when we arrived. The jumpers left the plane and I pulled the power and props back to begin the long descent. We kept the gear down and some power on the engines to keep them from cooling too fast and damaging things like cylinders and main bearings. I landed from the north, over the lake and taxied right up to the fuel pumps to feed the thirsty engines. As I stepped out of the door, I could feel the ground was a little too close and glanced back to see the tail wheel had gone flat. Okay, borrow a jack and lift the tail wheel up and find something to patch the tube with. Just as we were about to put the tail wheel back on, one of the jumpers walked up with a big smile on her face and informed me Charmian was in the hangar packing her parachute.

For those of you who don't know, Charmian is my wife. At that time though, she was still my future wife. I had been chasing her for a long time. I left Schaffer to finish the mechanic work for the rest of the evening. Even Dobergator had to entertain herself, I was not going to miss this opportunity to spend time with Charmian. All was finally right with the world. I had survived the disastrous summer in Seattle, the Lodestar was running like a top (the tail wheel was fixed), the weekend looked very profitable, and I was with the woman I loved. Nothing could spoil my life from now on, nothing!

Labor Day weekend festivities about to begin.

Charmian ready to load up for another jump.

The Saturday morning sunrise over all of those jump planes was a sight to remember. There were Beech 18s, DC-3s, our Lodestar, and several Howard DGAs, all waiting to be checked and engines started to begin a busy weekend. Pilots were crawling over the wings and checking oil and gas and pulling propellers through checking for liquid lock. Finally one of the DC-3s started up with a cloud of smoke and the old familiar sound of the radial echoed across the airport, then another airplane started and taxied up to the loading area. Did I say earlier that all was well with the world? I felt this is what I was born for. All of the airplanes, including mine were being readied to fly all weekend. The money we made this week would pay for the new engine, keep us flying for the rest of the busy winter season in Arizona and I was with my girl. I won't ever forget that morning, EVER!

Charmian and I walked over to the Lodestar and I began the preflight. First I crawled up onto the wing between the fuselage and engine and checked the oil, fuel and made sure all of the doors were securely shut. I did a careful inspection of the rest of the airplane. Back at the front I began to pull the props through all of the nine cylinders of each engine to make sure no oil had accumulated in the bottom cylinders overnight. With the airplane ready I walked over to the office for the pilot's briefing and to find out when we would start flying. If I remember, there were three DC-3s and four Beech 18s and our Lodestar. Each of us was given a slot for our first load and we would collect a manifest for each flight and present them to the management Sunday night to get paid.

Preflight check of the Lodestar at sunrise.

The jumpers were busy registering and teams of eight skydivers were formed by a drawing. This system allows the less experienced jumpers to jump with the "Sky Gods" and learn from their experience. It was great fun and people flocked from all over the West and some even from the East Coast just to be a part of this event. All of this organization takes a few hours to get together so the first load wasn't ready until about 10:00 a.m. By that time a good breeze had picked up from the south and word came down that all takeoffs would have to be in that direction. This would add five or ten minutes to each load since we normally took off north over the lake and landed south. I watched the first aircraft taxi as far to the north as he could and on takeoff he was several hundred feet above the picnic area at the south end of the runway. Two more planes took off and finally a load of sixteen jumpers approached the Lodestar, one of them handed me my manifest and we all loaded up.

Skylark Paracenter, Elsinore, California. Author is second from left.

This is how I remembered that beautiful day:

I strap into the left seat and turn on the master switch and confirm the fuel gauges match what I had checked visually earlier. Check props forward, throttles cracked, and mixture levers in idle cutoff. I peer out the right side and holler "Clear Prop." The fellow on the ground sticks his thumb in the air and rotates his other hand indicating I am cleared to start. I press on the fuel primer and then the starter button and watch the prop, counting the blades rotating on the right engine. After all cylinders had completed at least one stroke I press the induction vibrator switch and turn the magneto switch to both. After a shot of prime I wait for the sound of the engine lighting off. It catches almost immediately then dies, this is normal since I hadn't moved the mixture to rich yet. Another shot of fuel from the fuel primers causes the engine to catch and now I place the mixture lever to full rich. The engine dies again but only momentarily and the old familiar rumble of the 1820 cubic inch Wright Cyclone power plant falls into a steady cadence. Next, the left engine and it starts just as quickly. I've got oil pressure, temps on the cylinders and oil are starting to rise so I get clearance from my ground crew and bring the power up on both engines. I need to get up a little speed before I begin my 180 degree turn to the north so I can have the engines at idle when the tail is pointed toward the office where all of the crowd is gathered. One more check that the tail wheel is unlocked and I jam in the right rudder and tap the brake to start the turn. There is a loud squeal from the hydraulic system as the brake is applied and the tail swings gracefully all the way around. I reversed the rudders and ease up on the power to the right engine until I can taxi straight down the side of the runway towards the lake.

I keep a close eye on the runway off to the left. I have taken off from the south many times but this is the first time from the north. The desert is pretty smooth from the many years of use but as you reach the north end it starts to return to the normal sandy condition. There is no official end of the runway. We are expected to pick a point where we think it is still stable enough to safely support the aircraft (in our case at 19,500 lbs. right at maximum gross takeoff weight). I can feel the wheels starting to slow as the desert softens but I can also see tracks ahead indicating the DC-3 taxied further north and gained a couple hundred feet of useable runway. I wasn't about to leave any available runway behind this airplane and followed the DC-3 tracks, turning 90 degrees to the left exactly where he had.

It's time to lock the brakes and start the pre takeoff checklist. I use the acronym; Could I Go For a Trim Redheaded Female (named Char). Each of the capitalized first letter referred to an item on the checklist. C=Controls, free and clear, I=Instruments, check indications normal and set directional gyro to the compass heading, G=Gas, make sure you've got enough before you attempt to go flying stupid, F=Flaps, set them to 10 degrees for take- off, T=Trim, there are three of them, elevator at the top of the green take- off range to compensate for the full load in the cabin and the rudder and aileron trim set to neutral, R=Run-up. Check the oil shutters full open for cooling, Prop levers full forward for maximum RPM on takeoff. Carburetor heat check then off. Push the throttles forward to 30 inches of manifold pressure (MAP) and check all engine instruments. Next turn the magneto switch on the right engine to L and make sure the left magneto is operating satisfactorily. Turn the switch back to both then select R to check the right magneto. If you see only a 50 to 75 drop in the engine RPM you're good to go. Since this is the first flight of the day you exercise the props by pulling the prop levers full aft. As the pitch increases the RPM drops. Push it forward and repeat a couple of times checking for smooth operation. This also cycles warm oil into the prop hub, replacing the oil left there overnight. Now you check the propeller feathering pumps. There are two red buttons on the overhead panel and when you push the left one in the prop rapidly increases pitch toward full feather. As soon as you hear the pitch change you have to pull the button back out and the prop returns to high pitch. Repeat this with the right engine and now you've verified you'll be able to feather the propeller in case the engine quits. There's only one item left on the checklist, F=Final Approach, check the area beyond the runway and if it's clear you are ready for takeoff.

"Elsinore, Lodestar 1508 departing from the north."

"Roger Lodestar, you're cleared up, call us on your downwind prior to jump run."

"1508 is rolling."

One more check of the final approach and mixture, prop, throttles all set. Push up the power just enough to get enough inertia to make the 90 degree left turn and face down the runway, stop the airplane and keep both feet on the toe brakes. Reach down, rotate and drop the tail wheel lock into the locked position then slowly advance the throttles to about 20 inches of manifold pressure. I'm going to let the engines stabilize at 20 inches for about 20 seconds. This allows the cylinder head temperatures more time to climb toward the maximum temps they'll be at on takeoff and give me a few seconds to feel how the engines are running and check the engine gauges.

Everything is in the green and running smoothly. I and the airplane are ready. I ease off the brakes and slowly, steadily bring the engine up to takeoff power. The manifold pressures rise with the forward movement of the throttles. When they reach 29 inches the engines are at what would be maximum power for a normally aspirated engine but these 1820-56As are not normally aspirated. They are supercharged engines, there is a gear driven turbocharger sucking the ambient air and fuel though the carburetor and compressing it into the intake manifold. When we've reached normal outside air pressure of 29 inches there is still quite a bit of throttle left and I keep pushing forward, the manifold pressure increases beyond ambient air pressure toward full-rated takeoff power. The sound of the engines changes dramatically from one of a roaring lion to that of a bellowing herd of elephants. I get excited just thinking about what it was like to sit in between two of those Wright Cyclone engines at a full 48 inches of manifold pressure. They're cranking out 1,350 horsepower on each side of you. I keep my eyes glued to the runway to make sure this gracious monster stays in the center but out of the corner of my eyes the engines are clearly visible. The cowlings are vibrating rapidly and steadily back and forth, the glare of those ten foot six inch, three-blade Hamilton Standard propellers spinning at 2,700 RPM is faintly visible. The acceleration is increasing significantly and the desert runway is starting to become a blur beneath us.

I glance at the airspeed indicator every couple of seconds and compare the amount of runway left with our progress toward flying speed and the all important minimum controllable airspeed in case one of the engines quits at this critical time. This is the moment a pilot earns his pay. The decisions made during these critical seconds on takeoff are the most important ones of the whole flight. Make the right move and you'll soon be back on the ground ready for the next load and a beautiful day of flying, make the wrong decision and, well, you'll soon be on the ground alright, but the rest of the day could be very ugly. You have to be ready for the engine to quit at the worst possible time on every takeoff. It's not as easy as it sounds. After hundreds of takeoffs in twin engine airplanes without incident, it's too easy to forget there is still the possibility you will be struggling with this monster at full gross weight, low to the ground and just barely above minimum control airspeed.

Once you've set takeoff power your options at that moment are limited. You have to constantly measure the remaining available runway against your airspeed. If the engine decides to misbehave before you get to V2 speed (minimum control airspeed with only one engine operating), you have to reject the takeoff and stop the airplane before it runs off the end of the runway. In the case of a takeoff to the south at Elsinore, there is a 300 foot grass picnic area and a two-foot high picket fence just past the end. The picnic area is useable to stop the plane but beyond that is an elevated gravel road and then a trailer park about 4 feet above the runway. You have to be stopped before you reach the gravel road or there will be substantial damage to the aircraft and probably injuries to the crew (me) and passengers. The best you can hope for is that the gear will collapse when you reach the incline to the road and the airplane slides to a stop before reaching the trailer park.

There is a very short period during the takeoff that you will be in no man's land. The book says the airplane should be lifted off of the runway at 90 mph, 20 mph below V2. The acceleration should be such that the airplane will reach V2 even if the engine suddenly craps out at 90 to 100 mph and you will reach V2 so quickly that no loss of control will occur. You can then continue the takeoff safely if you perform several procedures correctly within the next few seconds. The airplane isn't going to continue to fly if you don't complete these few basic tasks almost immediately. The landing gear has to come up right away, then you're going to do a balancing act between keeping the airplane climbing or at least not descending while you try to milk the flaps up. At the same time it'll take all of your leg strength to keep the nose straight with full rudder into the engine that is still roaring with takeoff horsepower. If you are going to try to keep the airplane flying (your best option may be to land straight ahead) you will have to correctly identify which engine failed and pull the throttle to idle. If the good engine stays at full power you'll will know you have identified the correct engine and you can feather the prop. Once all of that is complete, you now decide whether the airplane is going to get you back to the runway or if you still need to just pick your best option straight ahead and take your chances. All of this is running through your mind when the airspeed reaches 90 mph and you remove your hand from the throttle. You have reached takeoff speed and only moments after the airplane lifts off you've reached the speed at which you have sufficient rudder authority to control the airplane in the event an engine quits.

At Elsinore you're taking off in a narrow valley with the Ortega Mountains on the west side and a smaller range to the east. Turning the aircraft around between these ranges 180 degrees, twice, while holding airspeed at 120 mph and keeping the nose up enough to maintain the 300 fpm climb (level flight) is asking a lot. There is a small airport 3 miles south of Elsinore and I had determined that, if the worst did occur, I would try to make it to that airport and land straight ahead.

Exit from the Lockheed Lodestar.

But, all of that has nothing to do with us now. We've reached takeoff speed, passed single-engine-control speed, and I am happily watching the ground drop away as we pass over the picnic area at a hundred feet and roar over the trailer park just beyond the end of the runway, accelerating nicely to 130 mph, our best climb speed. The gear comes up and the flaps are up and at 800 feet above the desert I slowly reduce the engine power to 30.0 inches of manifold pressure and pull the prop levers back to reduce to 2,000 RPM. As we pass over my alternate landing airport we're at 2,000 feet and climbing at eight or nine hundred feet per minute. Jump altitude will be at 10,500 feet so I'll climb to 4000 feet then turn left to a downwind. If the climb continues normally I'll only fly past the drop point a couple of miles and turn in to arrive over the airport at exactly 10,500.

Above and to the left I can see a DC-3 over the airport on jump run. He turns left after the first eight skydivers exit the airplane and levels out on downwind ready to line up for the second group. I'm climbing through 8,000 feet by now and call Elsinore on the radio and report downwind with the DC-3 in sight. Ground acknowledges and tells me I'm cleared to drop my first load behind the "three." I fall in line about three miles behind him at 9,500 ft. and I begin to reduce the power on the engines to begin cooling them down. The "three" makes a sharp left turn and begins descending after his load has exited. I love to watch the jumpers ahead but I don't want to get distracted from the business at hand. I've brought the power back enough to just maintain level flight and let the Lodestar begin to slow toward 100 mph. About a mile from the drop point I lower the gear and about ten degrees of flaps. Lowering the gear moves the aircraft center of gravity forward significantly. When the jumpers call for me to cut the power for their exit, eight of them will be as close to the door as possible. This moves the CG aft and the gear allows me to have enough elevator control to overcome the balance change and keep the aircraft from pitching up and stalling (that's one of the hard learned lessons from last winter). The old plane shudders noticeably when the jumpers race for the door and I bring the power back up and start a gentle left turn for the next pass. There is another DC-3 climbing on downwind below me and he is cleared in after we've dropped our remaining eight people. The second pass always gives the jumpers an extra 250 to 500 feet as a courtesy, and as soon as I feel the last person leave the plane I retract the flaps and let the left wing and nose drop to begin the gentle dive back to the airport. We've found that if we leave the gear down and accelerate to 200 mph we can keep a little power on the engines and still get down relatively quickly. The extra power allows the cylinders to retain some heat and hopefully keeps the temperature changes to a minimum. I do a 180-degree left turn, watch the DC-3 pass above and start looking for the Beech 18 that took-off a few minutes ago. Just past the airport I roll into a right 360-degree turn and spot the Beech climbing through our altitude. I roll wings level at a thousand feet above the desert and call Elsinore and report downwind. They call back and tell me another "3" just departed and I would be number one for landing and to park at spot three for my next load. As we slow to 115 mph I add approach flaps and let the speed stabilize at 100 mph and a 500 fpm rate of decent. The landing checklist is GUMP: G=Gas: both main tanks selected and sufficient fuel remaining. U=Undercarriage: down and locked, green light, and check visually by jamming your forehead against the windshield and checking to see about an inch of the main gear tire is visible. M=Mixture: set Auto-Rich. P=Props: levers full forward at takeoff position in case you have to make a go-around.

Over the end of the desert runway I slowly reduce the power to idle and let the main gear settle onto the dirt. The airplane decelerates quickly and as soon as the tail wheel touches the ground you can apply enough brakes to get to taxi speed when you've reached spot three.

As spot three approaches I am slowed enough to pull right in and happily there are 16 smiling skydivers waiting to board the airplane. I can leave the engines running as they start to load into the cabin. There are people all over the area to my left, they really had a good turnout this year. There's only one geek standing out there by the gas pumps with a tie on and I casually wonder what the heck he is doing out on this dusty old drop zone when Charmian plants a big kiss on my right cheek and hands me my manifest. I say hello and ask which load she is on. She is on the second pass and I tell her to pass the word that the second load would have at least a thousand extra feet of altitude. She says thanks and takes her seat to pass the word. As I bring the power up I can hear the second load cheering and yelling "all right!"

Another exit shot from the Lodestar.

Same procedure as before, kick the tail around and use differential power to keep the Lodestar heading toward the north end. At the end of the runway I notice a couple of airplanes had ventured a little further down than I had previously and decided I'd follow their tracks until the ground got too soft for my plane. I picked up about 300 more feet of runway. The run-up is more abbreviated for the second load and I let the guys on the ground and in the air know I'm taking the runway. I bring the power up to 30 inches and release the brakes. The old girl starts to move forward and I've reached about 35 inches of MAP when I hear the skydivers yelling for me to "STOP." What the heck! Oh well, pull the power off and ease on the brakes. We stop only 200 feet from where we started and one of the jumpers comes up to the cockpit to explain that Dan's reserve parachute had caught something and popped open. That could be a dangerous situation but I'm not happy about having to abort the takeoff. I can see I haven't reached the point I took-off earlier, but even though I realize there is plenty of runway it's an easy decision to taxi back and take advantage of the extra 200 feet I had just used. I unlock the tail wheel and kick the tail around and taxi back.

I call Elsinore and tell them what happened and they assured me the runway was clear and we go again. The familiar roar comes back as the MAP passes 30 inches. The old Lodestar is accelerating very nicely, everything is running perfectly and I am really grooving on flying such a unique airplane. The feeling of power and speed is overwhelming as the airspeed approaches 90 MPH and I am just beginning to loosen my grip on the throttles when, BAM, BLAM, BAM!!!!!

Oh Crap, the right engine is vibrating and backfiring loudly. I don't have time to even think about what to do, I just slam the throttles to idle and stand on the brakes. The old girl lurches forward as she decelerates and I realize that I cannot keep full brakes applied or the nose will dig into the runway. Gradually I ease up on the brakes until the nose comes up and I have to perform a balancing act between max brakes and nosing the plane over.

Damn, here comes the fuel pumps already on the left, they are very close to the picnic area and the end of the runway. That is when I first have to admit to myself that I may not be able to get this thing stopped in time. We race past the fuel pumps but the airplane is starting to respond to the brakes and the tail wheel is finally on the ground so I can now use full brakes. The picnic area is looming ahead and I am grateful that no one is enjoying lunch at this particular time. (I was told later there was a girl sun bathing and she passed under the right wing in a full gallop as I went by but I didn't see her!) Surprisingly, the deceleration seemed to increase as the Lodestar reached the grass but now I focused on the white picket fence ahead. There was no way I was going to stop before I went through it, but there was finally some hope I could avoid climbing up the dirt road to the trailer park just beyond the fence. It seemed like a miracle but the old girl did get stopped. The broken down picket fence was about a foot behind the wings but we weren't going any further.

The smoke was incredible. It flew past the cockpit until the south wind caught it and blew it back. I pulled the mixtures back and hit the kill switch on the mags and the master switch. I turned around to tell the jumpers to get out of the plane, and realize there isn't a soul still in here except me and I'm rushing for the door. The smoke was from the overheated brakes so I figured I would run through it (like I had much choice). I got about two steps from the door and I can't believe my eyes. There's a suit and tie standing there in the smoke holding up his badge and he's not smiling. Sure enough, he's a fed, the FAA, the MAN and I'm in deep do-do.

Now I feel like I had done my job admirably and gotten the airplane stopped but there is a hitch to this story I haven't brought up yet. Truth be told, at that time I really didn't want anyone to know this. When you fly an airplane that weighs over

12,500 lbs. you have to have a special type rating and I hadn't gotten my type rating yet. The reasons are many and I offer no excuses but that's the way it was on that bright sunny morning in Elsinore. I was in big trouble.

The Fed identified himself and said, "We need to talk."

I asked the Fed if he would walk with me away from the airplane in case one of the overheated tires blew and he agreed that was a good idea. As we walked out of the smoke, off to my left I saw a Chevrolet Caprice speeding towards us and I knew it was Bob in his girlfriend's car racing to the scene. What to do, what to do. It hits me.

The Lodestar threaded herself between 14 inch iron poles holding the picket fence.

I slap my back pocket loudly and exclaim, "Darn it, I've left my billfold up in the cockpit." We turn around and look at the smoking Lodestar and we both silently agree the plane is not yet approachable. Bob slides to a stop beside me and the right door swings open while the Fed asks me if I always take my billfold out when I fly. I stated that yes, I did. It is too thick to sit on all day. There's is now a look of suspicion in his eyes but I tell him my mouth is dry and I've got to get over to the concession stand and get a Coke. He doesn't like that but I assure him, "Look, I'll get my Coke and meet you in the office in 10 minutes with my license and I'll give you a statement then!" By that time I've casually sat down in the Caprice and Bob has floored the accelerator, the door slams shut, and we head for the concession stand. It's around the corner and down about a block, out of sight of my friend from the FAA so he doesn't see us blow past the stand at 60 mph and head out the exit of the airport.

"HOLY CRAP THAT WAS CLOSE!" I yell at Bob.

"Yeah, that Fed almost busted you!"

"I'm not talking about him. I didn't think that Lodestar was going to get stopped in time."

Bob asked, "Was it damaged when you went through that fence?"

"Hell, I don't know, didn't get a chance to look!"

Then he asks, "Well, where do we go now?"

I said, "Anywhere but the airport. What about that Mexican bar up the pass on the way to Perris Valley"?

"Alright."

At the bar we go over everything that happened and whether I should have kept going or not. One thing is for sure, if the engine had held on for one more second we would have been airborne and I wouldn't have a choice. The beer is one of the best I've tasted before or since but it didn't do much to take away the gravity of my situation. I knew one thing for sure, I could not go back to the airport until the FAA had gone home. This is a holiday weekend, so surely he had a barbecue or something to go to with his family. After the second beer I call the airport and ask if he's still there.

Three hours after the incident we cautiously approached the Lodestar to check her out.

"Nice going Mike, you missed all of those iron poles!"

The drop zone manager said, "Yeah, he's right here and he wants to talk to you!" I know he's handing the phone to the fed but by the time he gets it to his ear there ain't no one on the other end. I'm back at the bar, "Hey, Señor, I think we need another round."

"Si, two more for my best customers." This goes on for another three hours and two phone calls when finally one of our friends walks in the bar and he assures us he personally saw the fed drive off the airport, "Madder than hell, he was!"

A very close call. View from a porch of the nearest trailer house at the end of the runway.

By this time we had gotten up enough liquid courage to venture back to the airport. We circle around for several minutes but all we see are vans and derelict cars you would expect from our social class. I finally get out of the car and carefully walk to the Lodestar, always watching for my federal friend. I had no idea what I would do if I spotted him and he spotted me but it didn't hurt to be careful. There was no need to check if he had found my billfold in the cockpit, I've had it with me the whole time. The plane looked normal. It was still sitting half way through the picket fence. That fence was supported by steel pipes sunk into the ground and filled with concrete every few feet. As I walked toward the Lodestar I could see the steel pipe sticking up just outside of the left main gear. That didn't bode well for the belly of the plane. It was only a few inches above the grass, well below the height of the poles. When I reached the left engine, sure enough there was another pole between the engine and the fuselage; miraculously it hadn't touched the airplane. The other side was the same, poles on each side of the gear but, no damage. I remember someone coming up to me and complementing me for not hitting any of those poles. "Nice job!" he said.

I answered, "Sure thing, thanks." I hadn't seen any of those poles, the old girl had done that by herself without any interference from me.

Bob came over then and we grabbed the right prop and started to pull the blades through to see if we could tell anything about what happened. One of the cylinders had zero compression and we guessed we probably had broken a valve on takeoff. (That valve and piston sit on the mantle at my house today.) We borrowed a tug and towed the poor old airplane back to the side of the runway in the tie-down area and secured her for the long run. We had no idea what we'd do with her now, but Bob was actually optimistic about getting the other engine from the derelict Lodestar back in Arizona.

This is the valve that broke and damaged the piston causing the aborted take-off. It is on display in our living room today.

Lockheed L-18 Lodestar, N1508, back in Casa Grande, Arizona ready for another winter of flying skydivers.

That is just about the end of this sad story but things did get better. The fed turned me into the local Arizona chapter of the FAA but there was very little they could do. One of them was down on some other business and he made the statement that he had heard, "You almost got into some trouble over in California didn't you." All I could do was smile at him, there was nothing to say and he knew it. We did get that other engine and in a few weeks I flew the Lodestar back to Casa Grande, Arizona, and it sat there for a couple of weeks until I could get the examiner to come over and give me my check ride. It was an easy ride and everyone breathed a sigh of relief that I was now legal to fly her again. She flew for another year and then we sold her. I've had the opportunity to fly three different Lodestars since then and I've really enjoyed the experience but, there is one thing I know now for certain:

I'LL NEVER TRY TO MAKE MY LIVING IN A DAD GUMBED LOCKHEED LODESTAR AGAIN!

POSTSCRIPT: In the summer of 1977, we were pretty disillusioned about the future of our skydiving center so we began selling off the airplanes. That's really the only time we had any money. Bob had gotten his pilot's license and was going to start flying south and I had a job spraying in a Pawnee as soon as the cotton was tall enough, so we split the proceeds and went our separate ways. Bob got his multi-rating and was killed in a Lodestar accident a couple years later. I miss him dearly.

6

COTTON IN THE MORNING

The sun is so bright I can't see in front of me as the nose of the airplane slides toward the lush green field of cotton off the right wing. You have to be very vigilant in the turns this early in the morning when the sun is just barely above the horizon. I can finally make out the high school kid at the end of the field, his white flag waving back and forth brightly reflecting the early light. I let the nose drop and ease out of the steep turn, dropping toward him. As he sees me line up on the flag, he turns and starts counting off 30 paces up-wind (what little wind there is). Now the Pawnee drops quickly toward the edge of the field and my left hand eases the throttle back just enough and reaches for the pump handle. Because of the power lines at the end of this field I have to level off a couple of hundred feet before the edge of the field as low as I can in order to fly under them. Just before slipping below the lines I push the pump lever forward releasing the brake on the small propeller under the fuselage that turns the chemical pump. I can feel a small bump as the spray booms fill up and a heavy mist begins to follow the airplane across the cotton. Off to my right the crop is a green blur and I can see the mist of chemical from the last pass is settling in. The flagger at the far end of the field is already counting off his steps for me to line up on the next pass and I hold the airplane so close to the cotton that I can feel a few of the leaves from the taller plants slapping against the tires.

I love this flying but it is hard work. Getting up before sunrise and having everything organized so you can start just when there is barely enough light is tough. I still wouldn't trade places with anyone right now. Up high and to my left I notice a Frontier Airline jet on approach to Phoenix Sky Harbor airport and I know that guy may be making a lot more money than me, but he isn't even coming close to having this much fun. The power lines loom at the far end of the field and it's time to pull up over them. Because there is a barbed wire fence on this end going under these wires is not an option.

In quick succession, I ease in full power and pull the pump lever back to lock the pump brake and stop the spray. As soon as I clear the lines I move the stick fully to the right, almost full rudder, and the right wing snaps down. I pull back on the stick as hard as the airplane will allow, just enough to keep from approaching stall speed. This only lasts a second and I reverse the aileron and rudder to get into a steep left bank and start looking for the flagger for the next pass. I've let the nose go slightly above the horizon to bleed off just a little more speed in order to tighten the turn and my left hand is guarding the dump lever in case I over-do it. I know some crop sprayers who pull around a turn like this and hold the airplane so close to stall it buffets. I did that once or twice (only once on purpose) and I'm not that brave. It just isn't worth it, maybe that's one of the reasons I'm still here!

Here come the wires. I glance to make sure I'm lined up with the flagger on the other end of the field and can just make him out waving his white flag in the glaring sunrise. This time, I have to ease down into the field since I can't judge how high I am as easily while looking into the sun. As soon as I feel the tires touching cotton I pull up a few inches and hold it there. I can hardly see the power lines ahead but I know they are there. The poles are clearly visible on either side of the windshield but they are so far apart I think there is one in the center I can't see. I had better go over them this time. With a gentle pull the Pawnee climbs above the wires and there is the pole I couldn't see in the sun. The turns start all over again, this time to the left. After about ten minutes of this the airplane is getting light enough I can really wrap it around in the turn by pulling the nose way up and letting it sink back below the horizon while still in the bank and be headed back to the field in half the time. There is a flash of sunlight off to my left from the wing of another Pawnee going over the top in his turn about a half mile away. This is my last pass until I can refill the hopper back at the dusty strip about seven miles south in Laveen. That's home base, Bill Taylor Crop Spraying Service, Laveen, Arizona, I head back there thinking about how this morning started, much like every morning this summer.

Earlier this morning I arrived at the Taylor International Airport just west of South Mountain in Phoenix about 45 minutes before sunrise. There were a few flaggers already milling around drinking coffee and looking at the jobs Bill had listed the night before. I parked my old faded yellow '67 Ford pickup along the fence and walked over to the airplane I'm using and looked her over before climbing in. The Lycoming 0-540 engine was a little slow to start, maybe I had over-primed it slightly or maybe I hadn't primed it enough but eventually the air/fuel mixture was close enough to cause one of the cylinders to fire and the rest followed. I had pushed the tail around and pointed it toward the field of cotton on the south end of the dirt runway so the prop blast wouldn't blow into the bosses trailer house. Bill was a little hard to get along with early in the morning before the sun came up. He was always severely hung over from the night before and his daily exposure to the powerful chemicals we were handling made it hard for him to get started. Everything checked out normally with the Pawnee and I taxied over to the loading dock where I would fill the hopper with insecticide then move the airplane to the end of the runway and shut down to wait for enough sunlight before taking off. Starting the engine had awakened Bill and the light in the trailer house was finally on. I knew Bill was drinking his first shot of *Jack Daniel's Kentucky Bourbon* before he would emerge from his home and tell us which customer wanted his cotton sprayed that morning. Two more Pawnees taxied up and parked beside me and we all gathered round in the hot Arizona morning waiting for our assignments.

Finally the trailer door slammed shut as Bill walked over to his Grumman Ag Cat, started it up, and taxied to the dock. He stepped out and told the two kids how much to load into the hopper, staggered off the wing, and walked over to the three of us waiting for him. Man, he looked rough this morning. Bill was in his fifties but I couldn't tell if it was the alcohol or the lifetime of exposure to everything from DDT, parathion or some other highly concentrated chlorinated hydrocarbons we were using. Both were taking a serious toll on his health. He never made it through a season without being in the hospital for some kind of detox. We finally get our field assignments through a series of grunts and gruffs and hand signals from Bill while looking at a tattered map. Without so much as a good morning or be careful, he headed back to the trailer house for his next shot of Jack. It was still too dark to start so we briefed each other on what we knew about our assignments and waited for the boss to get to his big Ag Cat and signal the start of the day.

The door on the trailer slammed again and that's our signal to mount up. Bill walked past with just a little more spring in his step and a hint of a smile on his face and two cans of ice cold Schlitz Beer in his shirt pockets. He climbed into the Cat and started the old Pratt & Whitney in a cloud of smoke and waited for the light to improve and the engine to warm up. The Jack was starting to kick in.

Finally the big Ag Cat taxied past us and Bill throws out an empty can as he brings his plane up to full power heading down the desert runway. He disappeared in the morning gloom and I gave him just a few seconds to let the air and dust settle from his wake and I go. It was still way too dark to suit me, but Bill has a feel for this and there was always just enough light to start spraying when I reached the field every morning. The Pawnee cleared the phone line at the end of the 2,500 ft strip by a good 10 feet and we know when the temperature starts to reach 100 degrees we will not be able to clear the wire, we'll have to fly under it. I can see Bill heading northeast around South Mountain and then it's time to find the flaggers on each end of my assigned farm. It's hard to see them in this light but just as I passed where I think the field should be I spotted both flaggers in the dawn's reflection waving their flags. I rocked my wings letting them know I've seen them and studied the job site thoroughly. Nothing out of the ordinary other than the power lines on both ends. It was a nice long, wide field that will take about 6 loads to complete. That will fatten up the pay check this week a little. After rolling into a shallow left bank I aim toward the northeast corner where the flagger is standing and dive carefully into the field. The Pawnee was still too heavy to be horsing it around on the first couple of passes and that combined with the low light conditions makes it best to moderate my desire to turn fast and make more money.

After seven or eight passes I head back to Taylor International at 100 feet. On approach I tried to aim for the first two thirds of the runway at a 60 degree angle. This way when I chop the power and start the turn to runway heading the Pawnee should just about touchdown on the left main and tail wheel tire at the same time. The right main will come down as the nose settles a little to the left of runway heading pointed right at the loading dock. We're short of help today so the loaders are out flagging for Bill. I have to cut the engine and jump down to connect the hose to the valve on the right side of the Pawnee and open it. I step over to the pump and pull the rope on the Briggs and Stratton engine and it comes to life immediately.

Grumman Ag-Cat spraying cotton.

I can hear and see the chemical filling the hopper. It's easy to count off the load since the number of gallons written on the back and sides of the hopper were clearly visible. About three quarters full is all we can safely carry at takeoff. When finished, I ran over and ground out the pump engine to stop the loading then reach out, close the valve on the side of the airplane and disconnect the hose.

The Lycoming engine starts right up and we go again down the runway toward the phone lines. She lifted off alright but the stick still felt mushy and I'm reluctant to pull the nose up and climb over the wire. It's an easy decision to stay low and just pass under it before turning toward the job. It was already too hot to climb over that wire on the second load, this day was going to be a warm one!

Ready to head to another cotton field. The Estrella Mountain range west of Phoenix in the background.

This went on over and over until that field was finished. Every third load I taxied over to the fuel pump and added enough gas for another three. Sometimes we shut the engine down but generally I just leave it running. It's quick work, taking just enough extra time to swig from the plastic milk jug of half frozen water I left sitting above the old refrigerator by the pumps.

There's plenty of daylight now but that means it's also getting hot and what little wind was blowing at sunrise has stopped. Now we had to fly though the residual spray lingering in the air from the last pass. That means I have to use the chemical mask or risk breathing in even more than the normal amount of fumes leaking from the Pawnee's fiberglass hopper.

Before I realized I had to have a mask, I used to get high and even started slightly hallucinating after exposure to the overspray. After an hour of that I knew I couldn't fly everyday like this so I bought a mask. The three of us flying the Pawnees used our masks regularly, but not the boss. In fact, I stood next to him as one of my friends delayed his takeoff long enough to adjust his helmet and mask. Bill started laughing and mimicking him like he was adjusting a phantom mask on his face. He did wear a helmet for some reason but I never saw him use the strap. I used all of the protection I could. Even when it was so hot the sweat pooled in the bottom of the goggles and mask I wouldn't put them away.

We could work until about 10:00 AM when the wind and thermals kicked up enough that the spray either blew away or just got sucked back up into the sky. Then it was time to park the aircraft between the dock and fuel pump and fire up the Hotsey high pressure sprayer and clean everything off. We would spray the nose and prop, leading edges of the wings, struts, and stabilizers, and then rinse out the hopper. Everything just drained into the desert and I always wondered what it would be like to live around there after they built the inevitable suburb. It usually took about two cans of Schlitz to finish the job and then it was time to go home for a few hours and get some sleep.

I grabbed a 'to go' can of Schlitz, crawled into the old Ford pickup and headed out. I'll grab a hamburger on the way and at home I'll shower and be in bed sound asleep before noon. The afternoon is really the only time I get any real sleep. I have to get up about 5:00 PM to go back out to the field and help mix the chemical for the next morning. That takes until just after dark so, after a few more cans of beer, we can go home again and socialize with the family until their bedtime. At night, I sleep very lightly. Even though I showered again that evening, the residual smell from the chemicals is over-powering. Just when I start to doze off, the chemicals effects kick in and my leg starts shaking or I'll break into a cold sweat and wake up again. I'll check the clock then try to sleep some more.

I complained about this to Bill once and he informed me I was not drinking enough. What I wasn't drinking enough of, he wouldn't define, but I think I know. He just laughed and said, "Well, if we were just watering flowers it would be the perfect job wouldn't it." I couldn't really argue with him, the exposure to the chemicals is just part of the job.

By late July, after the second month, we were all getting fatigued and a little casual about the job. We hadn't had any serious incidents and everything started to seem routine. It was almost like any job now. The flying didn't seem to be as much fun. The chemicals were taking its toll, and some of the annoyances that were trivial early in the season seemed to take on renewed significance. Bill had already been in the hospital for a few days but was back to drinking and flying as usual.

I watched one morning as he was trying to unplug a clogged nozzle on his boom. He banged on it with his pliers (we all carried them in our pocket) then figured out he would have to unscrew it to clean it out. He looked around and found an open five gallon can that was still two thirds full of chlorinated hydrocarbon concentrate. He carried it over to the plane, sat it under the leaking nozzle, unscrewed the nozzle, but he was shaking from the chemicals and booze so badly the pliers dropped into the can of chemical. He looked around to find something to fish it out with but didn't see anything handy so he just shrugged his shoulders and reached into the can with his bare hand. He blew on the nozzle and that seemed to clear the clog, screwed it back on the boom, and walked over to the irrigation canal and rinsed his arm. He was back in the hospital two days later.

Bill always had a girlfriend who could look after things when he was sick but her most important job was to bring his bottle of Jack to him when he was in the hospital. The two of them would get soused every night there instead of the local dive until Bill could be discharged and get back to the job at hand.

It was early August now and the season was getting busier and busier. Sometimes we had to come out in the evening to finish up spraying some of the fields we couldn't get to that morning before it got too hot. In that case, we were mixing until well after midnight to get ready for the morning. I sometimes wondered why I even went home. I could never have done this job without the support of my wife. She would even come out some mornings and flag for me if Bill couldn't locate enough kids, Mexicans or Indians.

I remember one morning coming out of a turn after a spray pass and seeing two Indians walking along the canal where Charmian was flagging. On the next pass, I saw they had stopped and were trying to talk to her. She was stepping off her paces to get out of my way and the Indians followed about 25 feet behind. I've often wondered if they got sick from the spray I dumped on them as I went over. I was so low they barely had time to belly into the canal. I pulled up and reduced power to land on the canal road but when I came out of the turn they were half walking, half running past Charmian to get clear of the area.

Of course, since this was Bill Taylor's operation he sprayed all of the best fields and always flew the Ag Cat. Nobody begrudged him that, it's the way of the world. My field was a pretty good one the next day. It was just between Sky Harbor Airport and South Mountain and I would be in it for a good two hours. As luck would have it, Bill was working about a quarter mile south of me and I would watch him flying that big Cat when

I could. He was a master at it. From behind, you could see all four ailerons in full deflection in perfect coordination with the rudder as he rolled the old girl back and forth. Up and down he would go, disappearing behind the houses lining the north side and then up over the power lines on the other end and into another steep turn. I envied his skill and I wanted to fly an Ag Cat someday. I knew there would be more money made in that airplane than in the Pawnee. I came out of my turn on the east end and took another glance at Bill but he wasn't in the field any longer and I figured he must have finished up and gone back to the airport. Later, after my day was finished I heard the story from the loaders.

Author after loading fuel at the pump. Every third load we had to refill with avgas.

Bill was down in the field going full blast when he noticed a humming noise coming from the engine. The humming quickly progressed to a slight squeal which progressed to a loud squeal accompanied by a vibration that became very annoying. By this time he had stopped spraying and pulled the airplane up above the cotton and started a right turn back to home. Unfortunately, the squeal in the engine suddenly stopped when the propeller screeched and stopped turning. The engine had frozen up. Bill was high enough to clear the power lines along Baseline Road on the south end so he dropped the nose and right in front of him was a short gravel road that was climbing up South Mountain. He slapped the wheels onto the gravel and slammed on the brakes to get her stopped. He said it was awfully quiet when he got out of the airplane. He could hear birds chirping, lizards running through the desert, and the engine crackling as it cooled. He looked the engine over and there wasn't any visible damage on the outside, since it had cooled considerably he found that he could move the prop with a little effort and it didn't take long to figure out what had happened. He confirmed there was no oil showing on the dip stick and then checked the prop again and it turned normally. He surmised everything should be alright if he just put some oil in the tank. He had stopped perpendicular to a driveway leading to a house and by this time a housewife was standing on the porch looking worriedly at the airplane parked next to her front yard. She couldn't understand how the right wing had missed her mailbox. Bill smiled and asked if he could use the phone. She asked if she needed an ambulance or the authorities, but Bill laughed and explained everything was okay, he just needed to call and have his boys bring him some oil, he had after all, only made a precautionary landing to check something.

This satisfied the lady and she let him in to use the phone. Bill did have a way with the ladies. His current girlfriend and office manager answered the phone and she wrote on her pad what Bill ordered. He wanted seven gallons of 120 weight oil and two six packs of Schlitz delivered to this address and pronto! The loaders promptly gathered everything and drove at breakneck speed to the scene. Once there Bill told them to fill the oil tank and give him the beer. They emptied the oil into the tank as quickly as they could while Bill sat in the truck working on the Schlitz. These guys filled the tank of the Ag Cat in record time, but they weren't fast enough. By the time they were finished there wasn't any beer left for their trip back to the airport. Bill had them turn the Cat around and then push it as far up the hill as they could (they only had about 100 feet to go). He then hopped into the cockpit, started the engine, roared past the house, smiling and waving to his host on the porch. He made a bee line for the airport. Once there, he left the airplane next to the Hotsey pressure sprayer and walked into his trailer house and passed out for the rest of the morning.

Grumman Ag-Cat.

That's how I got to fly the Ag Cat that season. While Bill was asleep, I finished cleaning my Pawnee and then started to work on the Cat. I cleaned her off as best I could and then started to check the engine. First thing was the oil screen. It was clear. I checked the compression on the cylinders then drained the new oil into a bucket and checked it out then poured it back into the tank. Everything seemed fine to me. I had a lot of time sitting between those old Pratts over the years flying a Twin Beech and

I knew the engine was almost indestructible. After doing a run up and checking everything again I called Bill and told him it seemed fine and he should be able to fly the airplane again tomorrow. He already knew the airplane was going to fly again tomorrow, what he wasn't sure about, until I called him, was who was going to fly the airplane tomorrow. My phone call settled the question. He told me since I cared enough about the airplane to do what I had done that afternoon, that I could fly it the rest of the season. It wasn't really that big of a surprise. It had been pretty obvious in the last few days Bill had about had it for the summer and he was looking for a way to stand down for the season. I was so happy, I disregarded any reservations I harbored about the engine and eagerly showed up the next morning, ready to go.

About three weeks later I grounded the Ag Cat for the rest of the season. Not because of the engine, it ran for several more years. Bill was a little more careful about how much oil was left in the tank. I took it through a set of power lines at Bill's biggest account. We lost the account over it but that was really a relief. One of our guys had lost track of how many loads he had flown since fueling and the engine quit on his last pass in the field. He was alright, the Pawnee would protect the pilot in an accident, but both main gears collapsed and the airplane and pilot were done for the season. That really overloaded the rest of us until I lost that account.

My accident was, of course, on the very first load of the morning. The fields were lined up so closely that you could spray for almost two miles, just pulling up over the wires between them. I counted them as I flew the first pass with the sun behind me then, pulled up and turned the two thirds full Ag Cat around and fell back into the field a little uneasy. It was hard to see anything up ahead. I thought I had two fields to spray before the power lines, but it was only one. There was no time to do anything but slam the throttle forward when I saw the line and the sound of the crash was deafening. The Cat lurched toward the cotton and I yanked back on the elevator just as the line broke. That was a relief until I realized that the line was half wrapped around the right strut and I was yawing sharply to the right. Even with full left aileron and rudder we were starting to slide lower and to the right but the line finally played out and the old airplane leaped up out of the cotton and started climbing. I took stock of the airplane and realized I still had to hold about half left aileron and rudder to keep heading back to Taylor Intl. The right struts were bent back slightly more than the left, but she was flying and I was going to make it back. Bill was pretty pissed when I got there, almost like he had never gone through a set of wires. We drained the chemical back into the tank and he sent me over to the old Pawnee and told me to go finish up.

It was a relief when the cotton was ready for defoliation and we could get away from the nasty chemicals. That signaled the end of the season and except for a few fertilizing and planting jobs with a spreader I was done. Surprisingly, Bill told me I would still have a seat in the Pawnee the next summer but I knew I wasn't coming back because of the phone call I had received a week earlier.

That day I had flown my most profitable morning all season. While I was cleaning the Pawnee the phone rang in the office. I was the only one around so I answered and it was my friend Randy Roach calling. Randy had flown for us when the parachute center was at its peak and after he graduated from college he sprayed for a couple of seasons then negotiated a DC-8 flight engineer rating. It cost him a lot of money. He did get a job as a DC-8 engineer at Willow Run Airport in Ypsilanti, MI. He had just completed an overnight flight delivering auto parts to a GM plant in Oakland, California, and he bragged about how much money he made. He had made twice as much as I had that day while sitting on his duff drinking coffee and listening to dirty jokes all night and here I was pressure washing parathion off an old Pawnee.

That did it. Spraying wasn't as much fun from that point on. Randy and I ended our conversation with him assuring me he would get me in the door if I could just do three things. One, I needed an instrument rating. Two, I would need an A&P license. Three, I would have to buy a DC-8 flight engineer ticket like he did. That was a tall order but it seemed worth it to me and I started taking instrument instruction the next week.

That began a career flying airliners for the next 27 years. I enjoyed that flying immensely but on occasion, on final approach to the Phoenix Sky Harbor Airport I would notice a flash of sun light reflecting from the wings of a Pawnee spraying cotton south of the airport. For a split second I would think about trading places with that pilot but just for a split second, THAT WAS LIVING, but those days are over.

7

C'MON, LET'S GO FLYING

It was late in 1998 and things were going pretty well at the Larson household. I was talking to a friend who was looking for his own airplane.

Mike and Charmian Larson over Estes Park, Colorado.

Tom wanted a Bonanza but I casually made the statement that I would rather have a Cessna 195. Prior to this conversation

I hadn't even considered that I would want to own an airplane again. I get plenty of flying at the airline I work for (Continental Airlines) and for the last 11 years had always made jokes about airline pilots who owned airplanes. It had been over 20 years since I'd owned or even flown a small plane and I figured I was doing just fine without one.

I learned to fly in 1964 in Denver, Colorado, and spent 15 years trying to make a living flying small planes. For seven of those years all I did was fly skydivers in C-180s, B-18s, and an old Lockheed Lodestar. For the last three years we even had a '49 C-195 and that is when I learned to love one of the finest airplanes ever built. I used to fly that airplane everyday commuting between Phoenix and Casa Grande, Arizona, and then fly a few loads of jumpers before commuting back to Skyharbor Airport. On weekends we'd fly the Beech and Lodestar and Cessna up and down until sunset and occasionally till late at night. Needless to say, Monday morning we had to start maintenance on the old radial engines especially the 1820s on the Lodestar, occasionally the 985s on the Beech's but old shaky (the Jacobs engine on the 195 are often referred to as a shaky Jake) was rarely a problem. Climbing that 195 as fast as possible then diving back to the ground is a notoriously common way to ruin a perfectly good engine.

We did not have to change an engine or even a cylinder on that Cessna 195. I've always regretted the day we had to sell old 3451V but when we closed the parachute center, keeping a 195 for my personal transportation was just not an option. I took a job spraying cotton for the next three years and then deregulation caused some of the non-scheduled airlines to rethink their long-standing policy about hiring pilots who wear eyeglasses. I found myself in Ypsilanti, Michigan, engineering in old DC-8-23s flying around the country delivering auto parts. I had the job offer on Friday morning for a class that started Monday morning. That evening I was in the truck with half our household goods heading north. My wife (Charmian) and six month old daughter had to rent the house, pack up the remainder of the Larson's meager estate and meet me in Ann Arbor where we rented another house and settled in to a career of finally flying the big stuff.

In the three years of working for the airline (Rosenbalm), I was furloughed three times and moved four times. After working for Rosie for three years I spent four years running around the world at Arrow Air. Then I managed to get hired at New York Air in 1986. NYA merged with Continental in 1987 and I was able to move back to Denver.

Full stall landing of newly polished N8266R.

By that time I was convinced I'd never own another airplane. I was having such a good time flying those jets why bother with little airplanes. Except maybe an old 195 but they were way too expensive for me at the time I had the above conversation with Tom about his plan to buy his Beechcraft (he's since come to his senses and bought a nice 170). It was just a casual statement I made, brain in neutral and mouth full speed ahead. I didn't even mean it but Tom said, "OK, I know where a really nice 195 is available for around $35000," and I fell for it immediately. I said I'd buy it. I was really thinking of how much profit might be made if it was in fact a nice airplane. For two weeks I kept after Tom to go up and see if that plane was actually for sale. In the back of my mind I started fantasizing about flying a 195 back from California and I even thought about keeping the plane for a few months just to have a little fun before I sold it.

By the end of the second week I had actually entertained the notion that maybe we could afford to actually keep it for a while. I begged Charmian to just say no. I told her it was the dumbest thing I'd thought of for a long time, so please talk me out of it and I could get this stupid idea out of my system. To her great credit, Charmian didn't even hesitate. All she ever said to me was "Great let's get it!" Finally, two weeks later, Tom said he'd seen the plane and the owner and guess what? The price was not as stated. In fact, the owner said that he wouldn't even consider selling his beloved 195. The darn thing wasn't even for sale! I was heartbroken and relieved at the same time. Now I didn't have to follow through on my careless statement and I was off the hook.

That evening though, I began to realize that I was a lot more heartbroken than I was relieved. In fact, I realized that all I had thought about was owning a 195 for the last couple of weeks and the idea wasn't going to go away. I told Charmian the bad news and she wanted to know how much it would cost to buy a decent 195. When I told her what they were going for she was shocked. However, I then realized that she had been thinking about how much fun an old 195 would be as much as I. The only thing she could say was: "Don't you think you could find a nice one for less than that?"

Another flight over the Colorado front range.

Over the last 22 years that I've been married to Charmian, I have learned to trust this woman's judgment. This is a girl who in 1969 came over to the U.S. from England to work for six months and never looked back from there. She was around 19 years old, an unsurpassed beauty, and ready to live life as any youngster that age should be. I first laid eyes on her when she walked through the hangar at the parachute club at Columbine Airport southwest of Denver. She only had a few jumps at that time but she learned and persevered until she joined the ranks of the elite in skydiving.

Charmian was part of several world record breaking all-girl skydiving formations and competed in the national skydiving meets for several years. Two years in a row she won the national para-ski meets in Colorado and one year she was invited to New York to appear on the old "I've Got a Secret" program. Charmian learned to love airplanes during that time and eventually flew all over the west in small planes to and from different skydiving festivities. When we were married in 1977 we had a 1953 C-180 that we used to fly between Phoenix and Denver and around Arizona for a time. But, when we moved to Michigan in 1979 gas had finally reached $1.00 a gallon. That was the end of flying small planes for us.

Here she was, just as upset as I was about the hot deal on the 195 that went up in smoke. As usual though, Charmian was more determined than I was and she suggested that I keep looking around to see if maybe we could find one that would work for us. "I want one" is all she would say. Well, how could I look into those beautiful blue eyes and say no to that. Never have I been able to do that and never will I be able to either.

The search began. I talked to everyone who advertised in Trade-A-Plane.com and everyone on every website I could find. Finally I flew down to Alabama and looked at an LC-126 in military colors. She was a sweet airplane and ran and flew like a dream but I wasn't quite ready to buy the drab army paint scheme and the price was not negotiable. Ok, we have to come up a little on what we are willing to spend. Next airplane I saw was a blue and white beauty in Washington. This was one of the cleanest airplanes I have ever seen. She was parked on one of those grass strips outside of the owner's house and just shined and smiled at me while the owner and I talked airplanes in general and his 195 in particular over a Miller Lite.

The negotiations began. I made an offer and he came down a little, not enough but a little. My heart rate began to pick up. He's going to work with me. The 195 smiled at me some more and I raised the ante just a bit. He didn't say no! I knew I was on the right track, I could almost feel myself flying down the Columbia River on the way back to Denver in this beauty. Ok, time for a break, I had to go to the rest room and I asked him to consider my offer carefully while I was gone because I didn't think I could go any higher than that. On the way back upstairs I was confident that we were both in the ballpark and a deal was about to be struck.

Wait a minute, what's that noise? I could hear a voice on a telephone answering machine and it said something like: "I'm still interested in your beautiful 195 you showed me. Give me a call so we can talk." Needless to say all negotiations stopped at that point and I was soon in my rental car heading back to the hotel having lost the deal. The gentleman on the answering machine, I was told later, did in fact buy the plane and we were very close in price. I believe he took her back to Atlanta and I offer my congratulations to the new owner of that fine blue and white clean 195.

One of the first calls I had made about buying a 195 was to Goodland, Kansas to a fellow named John Collett. John runs Butterfly Aviation and there he and his guys rebuild 195s when the local sprayers don't have them busy working on their airplanes. John talked to me for over an hour about the plane he had just rebuilt and was just about ready to finish her up. The price was a little high for our finances but that didn't stop John from spending his valuable time with me offering words of wisdom and kind encouragement about joining the ranks of proud 195 drivers. The next week after the disappointing Seattle experience I decided to make the three-and-one-half-hour drive from Denver to Goodland just to talk to the experts and take a look at John's project.

It was kind of a blustery February day, not real cold and not real windy but wintry just the same. I arrived right around lunch and as I walked into the hangar old 66R was tucked behind several sprayers in various stages of winter repair and modification. She was stripped of all the old paint and partially polished and looked at me with a longing in her heart I'll never forget. When I walked around her I could hear her say: "Come on, let's go flying, you don't need the little bit of money you'll have to give to own me. You'll be glad to be rid of it!"

N8266R just east of Long's Peak, Colorado.

I resisted. It wasn't easy but I had only come out here to learn more about 195s and I wasn't about to get caught up in the temptations of some airplane that hadn't even flown for over four years. The next thing I know I'm in John's office making an offer. I wanted that airplane. The offer was ridiculously low and I knew it and John knew it but we both knew it was a starting point. Negotiating for something like a 195 is a bit of a stressful undertaking. The seller knows you want the darn thing and so do you and you know you are going to pay a lot of money for it. The only question is how much. Really, how much isn't as important as you first think. More important is finding where the bottom line between the seller and the amount of money you actually have is going to fall. Neither party really knows what those figures actually are until the deal is done.

When I left Denver there was no way I could come up with the kind of money it would take to buy 66R from John. She had a brand new 300hp Jacobs engine rebuilt in 1994 in Page, Arizona, a newly overhauled prop, new annual, and more than I could imagine I'd want in the 195 for us. When I looked into the cowling at that new blue case on that old Jacobs engine my knees began to shake. My heart rate and blood pressure increased a good 50%. You can't make rational decisions when you are in such a state of mind and that's why I was sitting across the desk from John saying foolish things about an airplane that was perfect in every way. Thank goodness John Collett is a rational and patient man. He must have sat here dozens of times with other 195 wannabes and patiently explained to them that he understands their concerns and reservations but he will not be giving you a perfectly wonderful airplane just because you want it. I can't believe he didn't just throw me out of his office.

We spent over an hour talking about 66R and her history and her future (which, by the end of our conversation, wasn't going to include me). I left Goodland and 66R in the hangar but my head was still dizzy from the experience. I learned more about 195s that afternoon with John and his guys than I had in the whole three years I had owned one. The three-and-a-half-hour drive went by quickly as I thought about all of the information I was trying to absorb. That old 1949 195 that John had put together is going to be a nice airplane for someone and why not Charmian and me? That night we talked it over and came, once again, to the decision that maybe we ought to spend a little more and get a top quality airplane that we could keep for a long time.

I called John the next morning and we found the middle ground that had eluded us the day before and the agreement was made. I sent a down payment and John set about finishing the airplane with the paint design (original) and getting the airworthiness certificate back on the old bird. I was ready to go back to Goodland the next day to pick her up but as everyone knows, these things take time. February passed into March and April was approaching as John and I kept in close contact about the progress. Sometimes I'd call just to hear what progress had been made even though I knew that it would not be much. At times like this I would talk to Marilyn, John's wife and partner at Butterfly. I was just thankful for the friendly reassurance from anyone at Butterfly about how the project was going. They are a friendly group out there.

Taking off from Eire Airpark, Colorado.

Throughout this whole time I never felt like I was being a pest (even though I was) nor were any of my questions or concerns ever ignored. If one is in a business like this, one should try to do it like John and Marilyn do it. We finally agreed that the airplane was ready in early April except for the interior and since the headliner was already installed we would pick up the plane before the rest of the interior arrived and come back later to finish. My next days off were three days away so I was anxious to get going. John had agreed to fly with me to get me back up to speed flying a tail dragger and I had rented a Decathlon and instructor for an hour just to get my feet back into the water.

Mid-April in Colorado is not always the best for flying. In fact the weather in February and March are sometimes better than in April and May. I've always turned around the old cliché about March and said the weather in March comes in like a lamb and out like a lion. The lion invariably continues through April and on into May.

Over Estes Park, Colorado, all Cessna 195 photos in this chapter courtesy of: George Weaver.

Naturally, my days off fell on a good old Colorado spring snowstorm. I went back to work again until the next weeks days off but there was another storm coming through then as well but this one moved through faster than forecast and Sunday afternoon I caught a commuter flight to Goodland. John met me at the hangar and took me around the patch one time and then we switched seats and I was finally back at the controls of a 195. I have to tell you it was not as comfortable as I remembered it. I guess in 20 years you forget a lot and I had forgotten most of it. I kept trying to flare up around 20 feet the first few landings but John kept coaching me until it started to come back. We had to head for the hangar because of a storm moving in from the west. I certainly didn't feel ready to fly back to Denver that evening so John invited me to his house for the evening and then fixed me an egg sandwich for dinner and we had a wonderful evening talking airplanes and solving the world's problems.

Monday morning dawned with thick low fog but it cleared by the time we finished breakfast at the airport café and we rolled 66R out for a few more touch and goes. Everything went smoothly so we refueled and said our goodbyes and I headed west. The rest of the story is still taking place. We've flown 66R for about 50 hours this summer and both Charmian and I are getting very comfortable flying around in a small plane. Not in just any airplane, though, in our own Cessna 195.

8

AN UNCLE'S GIFT

I remember that cool fall day back in 1952 in Wichita, Kansas like it was yesterday. I was six years old and I had just been told I was going for my first ride in an airplane. I had decided sometime before then that I was going to be a pilot when I grew up, but the reality of actually flying added meaning to that decision and I still harbor that excitement in my life today, 52 years later. All of my family were pilots so it wasn't unusual for a boy my age to follow in their footsteps. Uncle Mac was going to fly the airplane. He had the honor of being the first corporate pilot for the Coleman Company. His youngest son, Bill, was my age and he would be on the flight, we are still more like brothers even today. Bill, his older brother Mike, and I were the total membership of the Pleasant Valley Model Airplane Club back in those days.

After breakfast Dad and I headed to the Wichita Municipal Airport located next to the Cessna factory and McConnell Air Force Base southeast of town. We walked up to that beautiful silver and blue airplane and I remember the excitement mixed with wonder of what we were going to do. Yet, the closer we got to the airplane, the more I began to question the wisdom of riding in this particular machine.

Uncle Mac opened the door and I could see inside the spacious cabin. I distinctly remember thinking, *there is no way Uncle Mac is going to be able to see where we are going in this thing.* I opted to make a quick retreat back to the safety of the car. Fortunately, Dad had a firm grip on my hand and I found myself sitting in the wide back seat of that new Cessna 190 still wondering how Uncle Mac could see anything. I have only a few brief memories of the flight itself but that first impression has never left me. I've always been grateful to my uncle for that and other experiences he shared with his boys and me. It's one of those things you know that grownups are supposed to do and you always wonder if you could repay their kindness in some way besides growing up and staying out of jail. Mac flew Coleman executives throughout the United States in that airplane for several years.

After my wife Charmian and I bought N8266R, a 1949 Cessna 195A from John Collet in Goodland, Kansas, we waited a couple of months so John could finish rebuilding her. During the agonizing wait I had the chance to visit my 76 year old Uncle Mac in Atlanta and of course I proudly told him of our new purchase. Mac laughed and said "That is great Mike, let me know when you get her and I'll check you out." This coming from a man who hadn't flown in 20 years. Nevertheless, I vowed right then and there that I would fly that plane to Atlanta and get my check out.

After finally picking up the 195 in April 1999 and flying back to Denver, my first thoughts on that flight were, *What the heck am I doing in this thing!* I had been flying only airliners for the last 22 years and I wasn't used to all of the noises and vibration associated with running around in an old Cessna, and I wasn't sure I was going to like it. At that time 66R was a stranger to me and I really didn't trust her (or me for that matter). Having to skirt a few thunderstorms on a rough afternoon didn't help any! Approaching the airport I was glad the flight was over and I could think about whether I was really going to enjoy this new endeavor.

Uncle Mac running up the Cessna 190 he flew for Coleman & Company. Note; the crosswind gear.

I taxied up to the FBO and shut the Jacobs down and crawled carefully out of the left seat and onto the ground and began to stretch. The next sound I heard was Charmian saying, "Come on, I want to go for a ride."

I noticed a crowd beginning to gather around old 66R. Everyone was showing the proper respect for that beautiful 195 and I started to remember how proud I had been when we first bought her and how I was once again a 195 driver. My apprehensions began to drain away when I started answering the inevitable questions the airport crowd comes up with. Before I knew it, we were taxiing out for another flight. By then the sky was clear, the air smooth, and the pure enjoyment of flying returned. There were no more doubts from then on about our decision.

Throughout the summer we flew around Denver and used 66R as a lunch taxi for about 50 hours. I began to start to trust her and the old skills of flying a 195 were slowly starting to return. I still don't fly at night or on instruments but that's only because I don't have to. I am always amazed at the shape this airplane is in and how lovingly she was rebuilt in Goodland. I truly feel fortunate to be the caretaker of this 195 and the job is much easier because of the quality of care John Collet and his people took with her before I found her.

Our first cross country flight was to the Cessna 195 meet in El Paso, Texas in late September 1999. We left Denver around 3:30 PM and flew down the front range of the Rocky Mountains in almost perfectly smooth air past Colorado Springs, Pueblo, and across Raton Pass. Raton was a good place to stop for gas then we headed south over Las Vegas, New Mexico, to Moriarity on the east side of the Scandia Mountains, west through a low pass and finally we landed at Truth or Consequences right at sunset. The local airport bum steered us to a motel and Charmian and I enjoyed a drink and dinner before retiring to our room.

The next morning was gorgeous and we bummed a ride to the airport with the hotel manager. After preflighting the 195, I decided to file a flight plan into El Paso since it was such a large and busy airport. On the phone I explained to the briefer that I hadn't done this for 20 some odd years and he walked me through the process and gave us our weather briefing (clear, clear, and clearer in El Paso). Old shaky was running perfectly on takeoff and the air was smooth and visibility was crisp all the way.

As we neared El Paso I listened to ATIS and called approach control and told them we would fly south to avoid the warning area to the east then turn to the field. The controller gave us vectors direct to the airport and told us the warning areas were not in use that day. We landed long on the spacious runway and ground directed us to Cutter Aviation, the host FBO for us 195ers this weekend. One look at all the beautiful 195s on the ramp and we knew we were in the right place. We were greeted by the hosts, Larry and Ginnie Bartlett (I could not have guessed then how much we would enjoy knowing these two in the coming years) and started making our way to the office so I could close my flight plan. This was not easy, everyone wanted to say hello and talk about all of the beautiful 195s. I persevered and worked my way through the friendly group as politely as possible, trying to get to the phone before flight service sent a search party out for us. Once in the office I had to wait for another pilot to file his flight plan but finally he handed the phone to me. I proudly announced to the briefer that we had completed our flight safely and he could close our flight plan. He searched his board for a few moments and said he couldn't find us. I figured this was another example of bureaucratic bungling and I had simply been lost. So much for trying to work with the system. Finally the briefer found it! His next question was, "who had I opened the flight plan with because it was still inactive?" I asked, "Was I supposed to open it?" Deep down in the memory bank I realized that I had forgotten about that little detail. Twenty some years of flying around IFR and having this taken care of automatically had spoiled me. I simply assumed that everyone did it that way and neglected to activate the flight plan. The briefer diplomatically congratulated us on our otherwise successful flight and said goodbye.

We were not disappointed at the 195 Fly-in. It was one of the most memorable weekends I can remember. We met new friends and a few old acquaintances and learned a lot about our old airplanes. The flight to the Air Museum at Santa Teresa was great fun and the luncheon first class.

The International Cessna 190/195 Convention held in El Paso, Texas 1999.

The flight back was interesting since everyone decided to go back to El Paso at the same time and that overloaded approach control and virtually shut down departures since we were all crossing through the only departure route available that day. We had to circle around a power plant west of the airport before approach finally called and said, "OK, who's that circling the power plant now?" We identified ourselves and were cleared to the downwind leg. On base we switched to tower and got the last of a comment from a Continental flight that said, "Let me get this straight, you mean we're sitting here burning fuel at 2,000 pounds an hour waiting on a bunch of old Cessnas to land?" I did sympathize with my friend but I was having too much fun to worry about it.

After the banquet Saturday and the presentation about the Best Bar North of the Arctic Circle by Larry Bartlett (if you want to know where that is at, you will have to see the show) we reluctantly left El Paso Sunday morning and pointed 66R toward Houston where the airplane was to spend the winter. For the next few months we flew around Southeast Texas getting familiar with the weather and terrain and enjoying riding around in the 195. I had learned about polishing aluminum from Ron Karwacky at the 195 meet and I spent a lot of time at that task on the days I wasn't flying. The old girl is looking shinier now than ever before.

I hadn't forgotten about getting my checkout from Uncle Mac and in February the weather and days off came together and we headed for Atlanta on a Friday morning. We stopped in Natchez, Mississippi for fuel around 1:30 PM and called Atlanta to tell them we were about 3 hours out and would call if we decided to stop and spend the night somewhere. It was another one of those perfect days of clear, crisp weather and visibility. The vast forests and winding rivers of the South unfolded in front of the 195 for miles on end. We took turns following highways and railways and rivers. From our 1,500 foot cruise altitude we could see many details about this southern country I could not imagine seeing while flying along in a jet. Forty five minutes out I called Bill on my cell phone and even though we could hardly understand what was said we did manage to get the message across about our arrival time. We sighted Kennesaw Mountain just south of McCollum Airport and the tower cleared us to downwind. Turning final, the beautiful Georgia sunset shined into the cabin and that was a perfect ending to our flight.

That evening passed talking about airplanes and family and listening to music and just enjoying the warmth of close family members that you never get to spend enough time with anymore. Bill, Mac's son, and I had grown up living next door to each other for many years and we had a lot of ground to cover. We reminisced about Sunday nights watching "Air Power" narrated by Walter Cronkite and listening to my father and Uncle Mac talk about their experiences in the old B-17 and B-24 bombers they had flown. My dad flew B-17s, but that is a different story.

Uncle Mac started flying at the age of 15 at an airport not far from home in an old 40-horse Cub. At age 19 he signed up for flight training in the service and was assigned to B-24s. I have read his log books and followed his career through these documents and I am even more in awe of the sacrifices and dedication these men were asked to give during this time.

Mac had only 297 hours flying time in his log when he was ordered to fly a B-24 across the Atlantic Ocean to England to fight in the war. Compare that to what you were doing when you were 19. For me a flight from Denver to Wichita was a major undertaking. In a few short weeks after Mac and his crew arrived they were sent to Europe on their first combat mission. Each mission is carefully documented in Mac's standard-issued PX logbook. Mac also loaned me his precious few photographs that were taken during some of these missions. One photo is of a small industrial area in the country with a railroad, river and highway all converging, the obvious target. The explosions from the bombs of the 8th Air Force bombers have all landed about a mile out in some farmers open fields. On the back of the photo Mac wrote, "Spring Plowing." Mac related the details of other missions to me. The target was Hanover, Germany.

On the way over just short of the bomb run a mechanical failure forced them to shut down the number two engine. They knew the safest course of action was to try to stay with the formation. Unfortunately flack hit the #4 engine and it also had to be shut down. They managed to drop their bombs on the target but began to fall behind immediately. The flak had also caused the right gear to hang down at a 45-degree angle and the tire was completely blown off. As they turned toward England they fell further and further behind the protection of the bomber formation but soon three P-47s pulled in to escort them back to safety. They landed at a recently liberated fighter base in Belgium. The left gear held as they lost speed and the right wing dug into the dirt. The airplane came to rest on a heading 45 degrees off the runway and no one suffered any injuries. It took several days before they could catch a transport back to England and back to work flying B-24s. That mission was on September 11, 1944.

Uncle Mac's crew. Mac is second from left, bottom row.

On February 9, 1945 they were sent to Magdeburg, Germany. Mac has a picture taken on that mission and he wrote the following on the back of the picture after returning to England:

Oil Refineries at Magdeberg, Germany
River Elbe is shown
Estimated   50- 88mm. aa guns
    100- 155mm. aa guns

Really a lulu, flack, intense tracking fires
flack hit upper pushrod housing on #4

Engine went out on bomb run but managed to keep formation until over target.

At the rally point turbo on #3 began to surge. Lost altitude rapidly and was jumped by three FW-190s. Sgt. James W McDuff was killed by 29 mm. and elevator tab control cables were severed. P-51s arrived and we made it back to England.

The 100th Bomb Sqdn. a 3rd Div. B-17 outfit lost 28 or 31 planes 40 minutes later on same target. Jumped by 100 FW-190s.

Mac said the flak was indeed intense. The first hit was the number four engine which quit on the bomb run. Nevertheless they managed to keep the bomber close enough to the formation to drop their bombs on the target but the number three was also damaged and began to surge. Now staying with the safety of the formation was no longer possible and they turned for England knowing that they would be alone and sitting ducks for several more hours. (The logbook shows it was a seven hour round trip flight). During the turn the nose gunner spotted the three FW-190s heading their way. The FW's lined up and each began to make their passes toward the B-24. Sgt. McDuff was killed by the first fighter and the #1 engine was hit and disabled, the second fighter was unable to fire his guns for some reason. As the number three FW-190 lined up everyone in the crew hunkered down to try to survive.

Not a man would abandon ship. The enemy fighter started to, in Mac's words "Add a few holes," but then he broke off and dove for home as three P-47s sliced through the air and formed up on Mac and his crew again. The crew began to throw out any equipment they could to lighten the load and that's when Mac and his co-pilot realized the elevator trim cables had been severed and were unusable. On final, he ordered the crew to stand in the center of the bomber near the spar until it was time to flare for landing then they were to move to the rear so Mac and his co-pilot could get the nose up. All but Sgt. McDuff escaped injury and they evacuated the plane safely. That was Mac's next to last mission and he was rotated back home after serving overseas for a year and a half.

I could talk to Mac forever about his flying experiences in the war and then about making his living as a flight instructor at Yingling Aircraft in Wichita in the late 40s and 50s. Finally, the opportunity came to fly for Coleman and Mac stayed with them until 1964.

I've never been an instructor pilot although I have had the opportunity to check out pilots in Cessna 180s and Beech 18s but that was over 20 years ago. I have about 500 hours in Cessna 195s but only 100 in the year before we went to Atlanta, all from the left seat. I thought long and hard about whether I would invite Mac into the left seat of 66R and finally decided that if he asked for it, it was his, but he had to ask! After all, I'm the one who flew out here to get checked out.

Saturday morning was crisp and clear and we were at the airport by 9:30. We added a few gallons of gas and I busied myself with the preflight. While I was pulling the prop through to clear the bottom cylinders I could feel the plane rock a little as someone entered the cabin.

One cylinder always seems to have more compression than the rest and I have to pull on the bottom prop blade and really yank on it to get it around. As I straightened up again I could see Uncle Mac in the left seat intensely studying the 195 instrument panel and controls in preparation for our flight. I knew he was talking to her and asking if she didn't mind if he took the controls. Well, there was one decision resolved.

I climbed into the right seat and Charmian and Bill in the back. The old Jake started easily and I called ground control and we were cleared to the active. Mac pushed the throttle up and we were off. He taxied a little fast for me but we cleared the taxiway before entering it and there was no one else to worry about. I did the run-up and we waited for the oil temp to reach 100 degrees and then we were cleared for takeoff. There was about a 10 knot crosswind from the south as Mac lined up on the centerline, released the brakes and steadily increased power. Immediately we started to veer to the left even though Mac had full right rudder so he tapped the brake slightly and brought the nose back, a little too far and we were heading a couple of degrees right. Mac applied just the right amount of correction and slowly 66R corrected back to the centerline at lift off.

I knew he was talking to her and asking if she didn't mind if he took the controls.

Man, I was smiling from ear to ear as Mac expertly flew us out of the pattern and off to the north. This guy could fly, he was good. I stole a glance at my pilot and he was concentrating intensely on the airplane, remembering old techniques and various nuances only a 195 captain would know. But, through all of that concentration, I could see a tight little smile on his face.

But, through all of that concentration, I could see a tight little smile on his face.

We flew around for a while looking at the northern part of the metro area. Mac showed us the small factory he and Bill owned. A little further north we circled Mac's daughter's house then retreated for an airport west of town that had a north/south runway. I was going to make the landing and I wanted no part of the crosswind still blowing from the south. My landing was fine, not my best, but safe enough to get my confidence up so we taxied to the FBO and Charmian and Bill got out. Mac and I taxied back out for a few landings. Mac's takeoff this time was dead straight down the centerline. On downwind we talked over the technique he would use on landing and decided to do a full stop then taxi out for another one. We rolled onto final approach a little wide and corrected a little but not quite enough.

Consequently, Mac was still correcting as we crossed the threshold and he flew the plane on tail low and bounced up and to the left. He held the plane steady and when we touched down again he pushed the wheel forward and stuck the main gear on the runway. Mac brought the tail down and tracked the centerline on the roll out. On the way back out we agreed that had we been lined up further out on final, the landing would have turned out better.

Another perfect takeoff and this time we decided that after landing we could do a touch-and-go since there was more than ample runway. The line up to final was a little better but Mac was still correcting at the last minute, the landing much improved from the first but no one wants to quit until it's done right. With everything sorted out we retracted the flaps, pushed the carburetor heat in and slowly brought in the power. Mac had perfect control on the go-around and off we went. This next landing should be a good one and it would be the last since our passengers were probably getting bored on the ground while we were having all the fun in the airplane. At last Mac lined up straight down the center line prior to the threshold for a perfect approach. He had the speed nailed and just the right amount of power, he gently began the flare at just the right time. I was already smiling, thinking about that old saying, "A good approach leads to a good landing."

Mac slowly brought the tail down and we settled in for a perfect three-point landing but then, all heck broke loose. I'm not exactly sure what went wrong. One second we were just about to touchdown and the next found ourselves airborne again. Not just airborne but airborne somewhat sideways heading for the left side of the runway. We touched down briefly once more and bounced right back up.

Mac and I discussing the landing on downwind.

I remember thinking, *this is getting pretty ugly, we need to go around.* I hadn't even gotten the word "Go" out before I realized Mac had analyzed the situation in the same way and I heard old shaky at full power and we were safely climbing back to pattern altitude. It was so close to being just right that time and I was confident that even though the last landing may have been ugly, Mac kept her under control and knew instinctively when it was time to bail out. He lined up on another perfect approach, almost identical to the last one. This time I wasn't thinking perfect approach/perfect landing but I might as well have because that's just the way Mac did it. I heard a short beep from the stall warning and all three wheels stayed down with the tail wheel rolling along the centerline.

The Cessna 195 on go-around while doing touch and goes.

Mac knew he had nailed it that time as though all of those years without flying had never occurred. As we taxied in, a little more slowly than before, and as we neared the apron, I could feel the smile on his face and on mine for that matter. I couldn't help thinking about the time Mac had given me my first landing in a 182 and that I'm probably feeling the same sense of satisfaction that he must have felt that day long ago. I'll never forget that day and I can guarantee that I'll never forget this day either. Somewhere, down deep in my heart, I hoped that I had somehow repaid the gift of flight Mac had shared with me so many years ago, part of a long overdue debt that I am thankful for the opportunity to have returned. We walked around the airport for a while talking to the airport bums and the line guys then flew back to McCollum and put 66R up for the day.

That night the conversation was again about airplanes and that's when Mac shared his old photos of his days in the Army Air Force and then as a corporate pilot in Wichita. I was 53 years old then and had known this guy since the day I was born and I had never seen those photos nor had I heard the remarkable stories that were told that night. I am still awestruck at some of the things I heard that evening. The love I have always had for this man, my uncle, is now tempered with respect that I have always reserved for the aviation pioneers that we have all read about. Mac may not have written a book or won the Cleveland Air Races but he is every bit the hero as any of the pilots who did. His absolute dedication to aviation and airplanes blazed the trail that the rest of us could follow and made it possible for people like me to continue to enjoy a career flying airplanes in this free country.

The next day changed to drizzle and rain but still VFR so Mac drove us back to the airport to give rides to the rest of the family. On the way out Mac and I discussed how neither one of us really enjoyed riding in the back seat of airplanes. It seems most pilots feel this way. The first flight was full of youngsters and mothers and we did the typical sightseeing. The second was with cousin Susan and her husband, Michael, who had almost gotten his pilot's certificate a couple of years ago and he wanted to fly the plane after we got up. That left a lot of room in the back seat and as I started the engine I felt someone else get in the aircraft. With old shaky idling and oil pressure up I looked back as I pushed the prop control in. Sure enough, back seat or not, Mac wasn't going to miss one more flight in a 195.

Monday morning was raining and the ceiling below VFR so we had breakfast at the café then returned to the airplane. I called for a special VFR clearance and we departed southwest and were quickly into better weather. The flight to Houston was as wonderful as the flight out. We had to catch an airliner back to Denver that evening and at 35,000 feet in the 737 I couldn't help reflecting on our wonderful weekend. As I looked through the pictures we had developed I began to wonder, what is it about airplanes like the Cessna 195 that causes chills to run down my spine whenever I think about them. Cessna really hit it right when this airplane was designed.

She has the most beautiful lines of any airplane built and is truly a pleasure to look at on the ground or airborne. When you hear that Jacobs engine turning over as she passes by, no one can help but stop what they are doing and watch her pass. Then add to that to a weekend like the one Charmian and I experienced and there is no doubt about the decision we made to buy this old bird. I don't know if I'll ever enjoy a weekend like the one we just had, but one thing is for sure, with an airplane like our Cessna 195, I know that the potential is always going to be there!

POSTSCRIPT: We lost Uncle Mac in 2005, but his memory will always be with me. At the funeral, Mac's picture was surrounded with the medals he had earned in combat. I was surprised to see two Air Medals with four Oak Clusters displayed that day. Mac never mentioned these medals to me or his children and we were all astonished to find them among his belongings.

9

A 195 STORY

When I was 13 years old I lived in Sioux City, Iowa. One weekend in the fall Dad took me across the Missouri River to South Sioux City, Nebraska, to watch the air show at the grand opening of the Tommy Martin Airport. It was a wonderful and exciting afternoon for me. There was a low-level aerobatics performance in a T-Craft and then a thunderous demonstration by an AT-6 that was actually based at the airport. The afternoon began to go downhill for me when some darn drunken farmer walked across the field and actually managed to get into a Piper Cub that just happened to have the engine running. The ground crew did their best to chase this guy down but somehow he managed to get into the air. I was terrified. I frantically began looking for a place to hide to avoid the inevitable terrible crash. I couldn't understand why the rest of the family wasn't running for cover, especially my mother who was terrified of airplanes anyway. The farmer was down safely and the air show continued when it finally dawned on me that it was just another part of the show.

That winter, my friend, Dave Noble, and I would catch a ride out to Tommy Martin Airport on Wednesday nights to attend the free private pilot ground school. We would wander around the airport before class started and look at the Super Cub sprayers standing on their noses in the Quonset hangar and the T-Crafts, Champs, Ercoupes and Chiefs out on the line. The AT-6 was still there and a Navion was parked next to it. A little further down the line though, someone had parked a Cessna 195.

Hangar full of gliders, Cubs and crop-dusters at the Tommy Martin airport, South Sioux City, Nebraska.

As I mentioned above, my mother was terrified of airplanes. I flew with her only once in a Piper Cub. Right after takeoff I could tell that she wanted to be back on the ground so I turned around and landed. It took great courage for her to get into the Cub. When I was 14, I had to sneak out to Tommy Martin's because Mom grounded me from the airport until my grades in school improved. I knew that wasn't likely to happen and I felt that even if they did, Mom would find another reason to keep me away from the airport. Every Saturday, Dave and I would search for leafs to add to our collection for a science project. We would have to take the bus out to South Sioux City because everybody knew that was where the best trees were located, right next to the airport. We'd get off the bus and walk the two miles to the airport and look for Tommy. I had $2.00 in my pocket and Tommy always took the time to give me a 20-minute lesson in the Champ or the Ercoupe. The lesson would go by all too quickly and then I would spend the rest of the afternoon listening to the pilots talk about their experiences. My science grade did not improve.

A little further down the line though, someone had parked a Cessna 195.

The 195 was owned by a guy who ran a construction business and he had a contract in central Iowa. He would sit on the porch at the airport and talk about the virtues of that airplane all afternoon. It fit his purpose perfectly. Every Monday he and his wife would hop in the Cessna and head east. If it was a clear morning sometimes I would see him fly by on my way to school. There were always pilots who would ask why he didn't have a

Bonanza or Navion but he was adamant that his 195 was the perfect airplane.

Not many people reading this would argue the point. The 195 is still the perfect airplane. There are several of the members of our 195 club who use their airplanes for business purposes today. It is just as reliable as the new aircraft coming out of the factory if she is properly maintained. When you taxi up to the FBO you can take pride in not only having one of the most beautiful airplanes built but you also are preserving a classic aircraft.

My wife Charmian and I take great pride in being Cessna 195 owners. It is expensive to own one of these airplanes, but I feel that aviation has given so much to us that the least we can do is take care of this classic old bird until we're ready to pass her on. In the seven years that Charmian and I have been traveling around in N8266R we have never regretted our decision to have one of these birds. We have met some of the most wonderful friends over the last few years through the 195 Club and look forward to any excuse to fly out for an event and spend more time with them.

High School buddy and fellow airport bum, Dr. Dave Nobel, with Mike on a visit to Sioux City en route to Oshkosh.

When we park on the 195 line at Oshkosh or Sun-n-Fun we are always visited by 195ers from all parts of the country and enjoy the easy friendship that surrounds this group. Sitting under the wing of a 195 at one of these events and watching the air shows and talking to friends is the highlight of our summers.

Jim and Val Slocum under the wing of a 66R at Oshkosh with Charmian.

The best part, of course, is after the show when the crowd is about gone and the sun is beginning to set. The beer is cold and the wine is uncorked and the hardest decision to make is whether to have dinner at ACE's or just go get another bratwurst across the taxiway. After dinner, pick a 195, there are five or six of them with lights hanging from the tie down ring on the right wing and anywhere from five to 25 people under the wing laughing and giggling about the almost ground loop or when someone finally admitted they were lost. The airplane stories and 195 stories told and retold every year get better and better. No one is ever called on how the story improved from last year and new tales may even improve from night to night. Think you don't know anyone under this particular 195 wing? Well, just bring your own chair and maybe a bottle of brandy and sit down. You'll find out you are best friends and if they are part of the 195 group you'll probably recognize some of the names from "hangar talk" on the 195 website.

They'll be interested in your side of the story so be ready to tell them all about where you and your bird are from and how you became acquainted with each other.

We spent an entire winter at Hook's Airport in Houston polishing and checking 66R so she would be ready for our first visit to Sun-n-Fun in Florida. I'd never been to either Sun-n-Fun or Oshkosh before, but now that we had a Cessna 195 nothing was going to keep us away. That was seven years ago and Charmian and I haven't missed either event since then. For months I would talk to the locals about the event, asking when they were leaving and which route and altitude would be the best. I agonized a little about flying the arrival procedure into Lakeland, Florida, but most people assured me that it wasn't as big a deal as it looked on paper. We bought a new tent and aired out the sleeping bags and tried to prepare for the adventure as best we could. Our friend, Tom Hinckley, would fly out from SFO a few days ahead of our departure and ride with us.

Tom and I met in the Air Force at Keesler AFB in 1967. I had just completed my first day on base and as I walked between the barracks I saw Tom packing a parachute. I knew where there were parachutes, there would be airplanes and we immediately became friends. After almost 40 years we are still close and share our passion for aviation whenever possible.

I was on call the day we wanted to leave but usually could get released early if things were quiet at the airline. We were ready to go by 3:30 p.m. so we taxied out with Charmian in the front and Tom squeezed in the back among the tents, cooler, and sleeping bags. We had to stay north of the Houston airport class B airspace and below 2,000 feet for the first 30 miles and for some reason just never bothered to climb above 1,200 feet. Beaumont, Texas, passed underneath in about 30 minutes, then

Lake Charles. Lafayette was off the right wing as the sun was getting low so we started making plans to find a place to stay for the night. East of Lafayette is a massive bayou that stretches between the Atchafalaya and Mississippi Rivers. There are no airports, cities, or roads along that stretch and I found myself flying over wilderness after dark, hoping that all the work on the 195 had been done properly. The old Jake kept up a steady beat all across the bayou and the lights of New Orleans began to become visible in the distance. We kept the Mississippi River to the left and finally saw the beacon for Saint John the Baptist Airport just south of the dike. I made a pass overhead and confirmed there was still a south wind and entered a left downwind.

It always seems hard for me to get used to flying below 100 mph in the 195 after a couple of hours in cruise. It's a lot quieter and the controls are more sluggish but I think what bothers me most is seeing the nose up high in front and the loss of visibility on the right side. I really have to concentrate to keep the wheel back and hold 80 or 90 mph until on final and then even slower as we approach the runway. We touched down with minimum excitement though and began taxiing to the ramp to find a place to tie down for the night.

We like to just takeoff on trips like this with no particular overnight destination in mind but sometimes you can really get stuck if there is no one around to direct you where to go. We did find a tie down and unloaded the bare minimum we would need for the night and looked for some kind of life. The terminal was completely dark and obviously closed, but in the distance we could hear a faint sound of music and headed in that direction. As we rounded the T-hangars, sure enough, there was one lit up and several people were milling around for some special occasion.

As it turned out, the owner of the hangar was getting everything gussied up for his daughter's wedding on Saturday.

We asked about hotels and found that the nearest one was 9 miles and in his best Cajun accent, Beaudrow (I'm not kidding) said he was just leaving and would drop us off. We piled our bags in the back of the pickup truck and headed to the Holiday Inn. Fried shrimp for dinner is always good but when you're just outside of New Orleans, it tastes even better!

We had arranged for a taxi the next morning and just before sunrise he met us in the lobby and delivered us back to the 195. How do you describe a warm sunrise on the Mississippi River?

The early morning was mist gathering over the river and drifted out across the runway and was a variation of a hundred different shades of pink, red and yellow in the rising sun.

The airplane was drenched in dew, dripping onto the pavement and the suns first rays were beginning to reflect off of her carefully polished aluminum skin and proud red nose. We pushed her over to the fuel pump and topped both tanks. Weather and visibility to the east was improving and convinced us we were going to have another one of those beautiful days. The Jake started on the first blade after I selected the switch to BATT and we were on our way again.

This time we headed south around the New Orleans class B airspace and marveled at the activity and industry along the rivers and bayous. We followed the coastline up toward Gulfport (GPT) and talked to the tower to let them know we were coming. Tom and I were anxious to fly past Keesler AFB for old time sake. GPT handed us off to Keesler tower and the controller cleared us along the coast through his airspace. As we neared the base I informed the tower that he was talking to two former airmen who used to be based at Keesler back in the 60s and asked how thing were going. After a long pause he answered, "Well, NUTHINS CHANGED"! Charmian looked up from the back seat and wondered what Tom and I were guffawing about. Biloxi Bay passed by and then Ocean Springs and we followed the old highway 90 past Pascagoula and into Alabama.

I wanted to fly over Bayou La Batri and the Roy E Ray Airport where I had flown and jumped during my last couple of years in the Air Force. The grass strip was still there and looked like the airport had expanded into the old watermelon patch on the east side of the runway. We used to get a kick out of watching someone land at Ray Airport on a hot Saturday afternoon and instead of taxiing up to the grass ramp, they'd stop on the east side of the runway.

With the prop still turning, the right door of the Taylor-Craft or 172 would fly open, then someone would jump out and run into the watermelon patch to pick a good one. They would dive back into the airplane as the pilot gave her full power and took off downwind with their prize. No one really cared who it was or bothered to try to stop them. It was too much fun watching the show and, well, nothing is better than fresh picked watermelon on a hot Alabama weekend. I ain't sayin how I know.

We crossed Mobile Bay and contacted Pensacola NAS to get a clearance through their airspace and headed back east over the coast. It was a beautiful morning and the beach already had several people enjoying the day. About 20 miles east of Pensacola I noticed a large round, dark spot about a hundred feet off the beach. As we got a little closer I saw that the spot was moving and changing shape from time to time and realized that it was a school of fish. There was a shark circling the school and every now and then he would turn into the fish and the round spot would collapse on itself and reform behind the shark. He did this several times while we flew over, but even more ominous for the fish, we spotted four more sharks swimming in from the ocean to join in on the morning feast.

Pensacola handed us off to Elgin AFB and they vectored us out over the Gulf to avoid an arriving military jet and then told us to proceed on our own, VFR.

We were starting to get kind of hungry up there and it had been a couple of hours since New Orleans so we picked Panama

City for our next stop and breakfast. The tower vectored us to final while Tom was flying, but he didn't want me to see his landing since it had been 15 years since Tom had sold his 195. I gave him a break and made a perfect touchdown just to show him how to do it. I regretted doing that because he whined all the way to the ramp about how he used to be able to fly, back in the old days. In Tom's defense, I rode with him recently when he made a pretty decent landing in his 170.

We found our way to the terminal and ordered breakfast and watched all of the airplanes coming and going. It was obvious we were getting close to Sun-n-Fun. There were all kinds of airplanes stopping in for gas and food on their way to Lakeland. The FBO sent the fuel truck over and we topped off again. I was pouring Marvel Mystery Oil into the tanks while Charmian cleaned the windshield and Tom was goofing off watching a Corsair do a 360 overhead and land. The Corsair parked right next to us and the pilot and his girlfriend climbed down off of the wing and gave us a friendly smile as they walked by. I walked over to the fueler to settle the bill, but he said that it had already been paid by that other bald headed guy. Tom had beat me to it this time.

Did I mention something about getting lost earlier? Okay, I admit it. I got lost that day while I was following the Florida coast. Impossible you say, let me explain. Everybody knows that the Florida panhandle turns gently to the south and becomes the Florida peninsula. As we left Panama City I began to follow the coast again and was pleasantly surprised to find that we were beginning to head south already. That seemed to put us about an hour ahead of schedule, maybe this 195 is a little faster than I flight planned, maybe we won't be buying so much gas on the trip after all.

If you look at the sectional charts you find that three separate charts have corners that come together in that area and not one of them will give you a true picture of the terrain. I didn't know Apalachicola was way down south in that bayou and if we followed the coast to there, we would have to fly back northeast. Last time I'd flown through here I was at 35,000 feet on LNAV so it took me a little while to figure out that we really weren't going down the peninsula yet.

Tom Hinckley attending Jim and Val's fly-in, Memphis , Tennessee.

When the coast suddenly started to head northeast, I had to admit to Charmian and Tom that we really weren't an hour ahead of schedule. I also had to tell them to relax, just because the compass is pointing northeast doesn't mean I don't know what I'm doing. It always amazes me how soon people forget about the good landings and turn on you at the slightest sign of weakness.

After another 45 minutes we were indeed turning south again and starting to fly down the peninsula. We were cruising along at a thousand feet, when I spotted two faint dots ahead. I kept an eye on them as they approached, they were obviously other aircraft flying a loose formation on the way to Sun and Fun. Soon I was able to make out the one on the right was a Cessna 150.

He was about a thousand feet right and 500 feet behind a yellow J-3 Cub. We were closing fast so I lined up right in between them and a little below and flew past them about 75 mph faster. They both rocked their wings when they saw us go by and I did the same.

We landed at Ocala, Florida to take advantage of the discounted fuel and review the arrival procedures and the Notams for Lakeland. We parked next to an all-silver 195 and met the pilot. He was a US Air captain and we decided to fly formation the rest of the way so we could park together. The arrival procedure went smoothly and soon we were taxiing in for the show. We taxied along a chain-link fence on the south side of the taxiway and people were lined up watching the airplanes go by. I happened to notice a fellow running toward the fence looking at 66R. Just as he stopped short, he held up both hands with all ten fingers spread out. I understood immediately that he was giving 66R the top grade of 10 out of 10. Maybe all that work back at Hook's was worth it.

We enjoyed the event and spent most of the week camping under the wing. These things always go by way too fast. Tom rented a car and drove to Tampa; caught a Southwest flight back to the West Coast. Charmian and I left the next day. We deviated north to Atlanta to see my Uncle Mac again and give him another hour in the 195, but that's a different story.

When we got back to Houston, Charmian and I took the cowling off to see what needed to be done after such a long trip, but I wasn't surprised that all she needed was a little cleaning and TLC and she was ready for the next trip.

***

POSTSCRIPT: That was 450 hours ago in 195 years. I've learned that I don't really need to take the cowling off after every trip to check things over, in fact, last year, I didn't have it off once between annuals. Granted it was a slow year; we only flew 75 hours. We've cleaned up all of the oil leaks and she seems to stay clean longer and just runs and runs without any problems. Someday I'm going to put a clean kit on her, and a JPI engine analyzer, and maybe even hook up the fuel injection.

10

THIS JUST IN!

A warrant for the arrest and extradition of one PATRICK ATKINSON has been issued by the Hog Jowl law enforcement committee in connection with the theft of a J-3 Piper Cub belonging to one Bob Jenkins (details below).

Upon arriving at Hog Jowl on Friday, Charmian, and I requested transportation to a facility where we could find something for lunch. Aubie obliged by directing us to a small store in the valley north of the airport which was conveniently located adjacent to our accommodations for the weekend. We then asked about borrowing a car to drive to the store and Aubie advised that we should use his newly acquired clip-winged J-3 Piper Cub instead. He further stated that a 1,300 foot runway was located across the street from the store. I inquired if the Cub had a GPS to assist in navigating into the valley and he said that all we had to do was takeoff to the east, turn left and, when we cleared the ridge, bring the power to idle. When the nose dropped we would see the runway right in front of us and 700 feet below.

Aubie's instructions were accurate and as Charmian and I were ordering our lunches, the subject of this indictment, one Pat Atkinson walked in for lunch, having been loaned an automobile to meet us. It was obvious that the perpetrator was agitated about being relegated to surface transportation and herein lies the motive leading to the alleged crime of theft of personal property.

WANTED

ON THE GROUND OR IN THE AIR

The opportunity to commit the alleged offense arose later that day when Aubie was approached by the perp under the guise of having to inspect the accommodations provided by said store in the valley north. Aubie, being the gracious host as usual, referred Pat to the clipped-wing J-3 Cub and gave him the same briefing as he gave to Charmian and me earlier. Pat immediately took off in the Cub and landed on the 1,300 foot strip to do his business.

Some of the airplanes at the Hogjowl Fly-in.

Unfortunately, as Pat took off, one very agitated Piper Cub owner, Mr. Bob Jenkins, approached Aubie and demanded to know who the heck took-off in HIS Piper Cub. Aubie explained it was Pat Atkinson but insisted he was indeed flying a clipped-winged Cub not Bob's J-3. Aubie stayed with this story right up until he observed a clipped-wing still parked in front of the hangar and the Cub owned by Bob Jenkins conspicuously disappearing over the ridge on the way down into the valley.

A discussion about the perp's abilities regarding Piper Cubs ensued and it was determined that another plane should be dispatched to investigate whether a Cub pilot of such limited ability could indeed land safely. The only other available aircraft was the clipped-wing Cub. However, a delay in dispatch was incurred while it was being used to offer rides to the airport neighbors in order to deter any complaints or legal entanglements. Finally, as the clipped-wing Cub was being readied for yet another foray into the valley below, the subject Cub miraculously appeared just below the ridge climbing mightily. It just barely cleared the trees, landed and, taxied up to the hangar. One smiling Pat Atkinson was accosted by several concerned citizens and informed that his crime had been witnessed. He still persists to this day his innocence of any intentional crime.

A summons has been issued and trial is scheduled at the next Hog Jowl Fly-in early November, 2011. All Cessna 195 Club members are also hereby summoned as witnesses/jurors during the hanging (proceedings).

11

TO FLORIDA WITH LOVE

I was grooving to Led Zeppelin's *Stairway to Heaven* on channel 46 of the XM satellite and watching the Louisiana countryside slip by as Charmian and I pointed the nose of N8266R towards Florida. We had a tailwind at 6,500 feet and the Atchafalaya River swamp was reflected off the leading edge of our plane's highly polished aluminum wing. Life in general and retirement with a Cessna 195 specifically, is GOOD! I didn't have to bid vacation this year for this trip because I don't have vacation benefits anymore. It's like this day after day and never a break from doing whatever we want.

We had learned in September that our friend and skydiver pilot, Charlie Kinlen, was celebrating his 60th birthday the first weekend in December, 2007 in Deland, Florida and we readily accepted his invitation to attend, pending good weather for flying the 195 to Florida. The weather cooperated and we discovered that leaving a few days early would allow us to watch the space shuttle launch on Wednesday. Who could turn down a trip like that? Not us!

I ran a flight plan on AirNav a few days before and found that, as usual, cheap gas along the Gulf Coast was going to be hard to find. There was this one airport, "Shade Tree," just to the north of Gulfport, Mississippi, that looked promising. The name alone gets your interest; it has a 2,800 x 100 foot grass runway. I figured I could keep the 195 straight enough to land on that, and fuel was available for $4.00-not bad for this day and age. I called the management, Danny Miller, and he said he would be on the airport that evening to meet us and we should plan to land not long after five p.m. if we wanted to be there before dark. After checking my DUATS flight plan it said we would make it in two hours six minutes with the forecast tailwind. We departed Hook's Airport at three p.m., stayed below the Houston Intercontinental Class B until 30 miles east then climbed up to 6,500 ft. Like I said, *Stairway to Heaven*, and I was *Feelin' Groovy* because that was the song before Stairway.

Charmian taking a picture of the Atchafalaya Swamp.

It's always good to lower the nose at top of climb and watch the ground speed and ETA update on the Garmin as you accelerate to cruise speed. It validates your flight planning and confirms that they don't have to turn on the runway lights for you when you arrive at Shade Tree. I looked over at my good looking co-pilot in the right seat and she was Feelin' just as Groovy as I was at that moment. I am extremely lucky to have a wife who enjoys the benefits of traveling around the United States in a Cessna 195 as much as I do. She is so proud of this airplane that she spends hours in the hangar below our residence cleaning and polishing right beside me.

Two hours passed by quickly and we began our descent. The airport is close to Gulfport and we wanted to stay below its airspace. I checked the ATIS at Gulfport and there was a light wind from the south. When I called Shade Tree on 122.9, Danny answered immediately and tells me it's almost calm. Grass runways are a little difficult to locate if you've never been there before, but the airport identifier was in the 496 and I manually entered it into the 530 as well.

We were about to go over the top of the airport displayed on the GPS when Charmian calls out, "There it is!" I am just over the north end and a shallow bank to the right reveals the Shade Tree Airport. Danny is still on the radio and he exclaimed, "Wow, what is that you are flying?"

He knows very well what a 195 looks like but since I didn't tell him we were flying one, I got the expected surprised comment as we went over. While taxiing back to the fuel pump the sun was just beginning to sink below the trees and the shadows were elongating across the lush green runway. I taxied up to the pumps and our greeting party waited for us to shut down while I let the engine idle for a minute or so to try to scavenge the oil back into the tank.

These people read the book on hospitality and before I could get to the fuel pump, it was turned on, a ladder was placed backwards over the left main gear, and Danny was offering to fill the tanks for me if I was too tired. In the meantime, Danny's wife, Janet, drove up in her Chevy and parked next to the right side of the 195 and asked if she could help load our bags into her car. She was loaning it to us for the evening. That's when Stormy, our six year old Doberman, jumped out of the airplane and started sniffing everyone in sight. Janet cringed slightly when Stormy surprised her, but she is a dog person and immediately made friends. She then pulled down the back seat of the Chevy and told us that Stormy would be more comfortable that way.

"That looks like a tasty leg bone or maybe I should just leave a little bomb to remember me by on that nice grass runway."

I put in 53 gallons of 100LL and then added the proper amount of Marvel Mystery Oil while Charmian and Janet were talking about life in general. Charmian mentioned that we had owned and flown a Cessna 195, dropping skydivers, in the 1970s and it looked just like our present airplane minus the polish job. Janet said they used to allow jumpers at Shade Tree but as the Gulfport Airport became more and more busy they had to curtail the operation. However, the fellow who ran the parachute business, Mike Brown, lived on the south end of the runway.

Wow!! Mike Brown, I've always wondered what happened to him. Mike was my jump-master on my first jump in 1967 right here at Gulfport. I asked if he was there now and I was given the airport golf cart to go down and check. Unfortunately, Mike wasn't home but Janet located him with her cell phone. When he answered the phone I went into my best "Wuffo" voice and asked about learning to skydive but he caught on right away and asked who this really was. We hadn't seen each other for over 30 years and made plans to meet for dinner that evening.

With everything loaded up in the borrowed car, I poured another gallon of W100 into the 195 and left her chocked at the fuel pumps until tomorrow. It was about a 15-minute drive to our hotel and soon after we were reminiscing old times with Mike Brown over a bowl of guacamole and a cold Dos Eque's Negra. Mike hadn't changed much except for age and we tried to catch up with the last 30 years in the short time we had. This is just one more benefit of being able to travel around our country in a small airplane and being free to stop anywhere you want for the night. That's a kind of freedom you won't enjoy anywhere else in the world (except maybe Canada).

Bright and early, at the crack of 09:30 we pulled in at the airport for the completion of our flight. We had skipped breakfast this morning in anticipation of a seafood lunch at Apalachicola, Florida. It would be another two-hour flight but there is a lot of restricted and high-use airspace along the Gulf Coast. We bid Danny and Janet a warm goodbye and took off to the south. I made an immediate left turn to stay out of Gulfport's airspace and climbed to about 1,000 feet headed east. After passing north of Keesler AFB I turned to the southeast and merged with the coast just east of Bayou La Batre, Alabama.

I swear I could see the Bubba Gump Shrimp factory as we passed over Bayou La Batre but I'd have to confirm it from the ground. I had made contact with Mobile approach and they kept a close eye on us until we were about 20 miles west of Pensacola, Florida. Pensacola was accommodating as usual but for some reason they would not allow us to pass by at 1,000 feet this day. We were asked to climb to 3,500 ft. and passed from there to Panama City and over the swamp into Apalachicola.

Again we were met by a friendly crew and immediately given the keys to a courtesy car, the one they reserved for customers with dogs, and given directions to a seafood joint that allowed us to keep our puppy by the table out on the deck while we ate. The meal was well worth the stop and we spent a half hour or so touring the town then headed back to the airport for the one-and-a-half hour flight to Deland. There was a $10.00 charge for the courtesy car, which I thought very reasonable when you factor in the cost of keeping a couple of these vehicles available.

We took off into the stiff west breeze and gently turned on course to the east. I tried to fly along the coast as long as possible, but there are so many islands and river outlets and curves in the beaches that I just kind of split the difference and kept either a road or beach within gliding distance. You'd think it would be easy to fly across Florida on a clear VFR day like this but there is more Special Use, Restricted, and Prohibited airspace in this area than you can believe and it takes a lot of attention to stay clear of it.

If we had been in a hurry, I might have gotten upset, but going around all of this stuff just gave us the opportunity to sight see along the lush landscape and swamps and lakes scattered below on our convoluted route. There also are many little fly-in communities and short and long grass strips that are worth looking at, some are on the sectional chart and some are not but it seems like there is always one to land on if the need arose.

Author Mike Larson contemplating his whereabouts on the Garmin 496.

The ASOS for Deland reminded us to beware of parachute jumpers over the airport and the jump planes might be using a runway other than the active runway. There is a fairly busy flight school and after listening to the Unicom we determined that we could fly over the west end of the runway and enter a left downwind and land to the west. We pretty much had the location of all of the traffic in the pattern figured out by the time we got there and fell into our spot on downwind behind a Cessna 172 and slowed down to match his speed. The parachute center is located on the southeast end of Deland so I decide to make sure I could make the first turn off about 1,200 feet from the end of the runway. There were two other airplanes holding short for takeoff as we passed by and I felt a momentary twinge of guilt for landing so close to the 172 in front, preventing any departures between us. As I cleared onto the taxiway I noticed that both aircraft would easily depart before the aircraft on downwind would be on final.

Stormy stalking a Great White Shark.

We taxied around the T-hangars toward the Deland Parachute Center hoping that we might be welcomed into the hangar we stayed in two years ago, but I could see that hangar was now being used by the skydivers for packing parachutes. An old pickup truck drove up and we recognized Charlie's smiling face and he directed us back to the tie downs where we shut down for the night. It was good to see Charlie again and it turned out this day was his actual birthday and he was about to celebrate with his closest friends with a jump from the Twin Otter in about 15 minutes. We unloaded everything into the back of the truck and latched the dog to her leash and walked around the T-hangars to the parachute center.

This place isn't like the parachute center I used to run. They have improved the business greatly since then. I was impressed with the facilities and how well it was organized to keep everything running smoothly. It was so well run that I discovered

I had only to snap my fingers and Charmian was in the Bar and Grill ordering me a beer (Yea, RIGHT.), but it was close. We watched a few jump loads and met a few old-time friends who are still active skydivers and reminisced about the old days over a few cold ones.

Charlie welcoming a rowdy crowd to his 60th birthday celebration.

Well, that's about it for the next few days. The Shuttle launch was delayed every day we were there and finally cancelled because of a faulty fuel sensor in the external tank. Instead, we used the rental car to tour the area along the coast as far north as St. Augustine and hiked and shopped until Charlie's birthday party on Saturday night. He keeps his Cessna 170 at the Deep Woods Airport about 18 miles west of Deland. At dinner the night before, I kept begging Charlie to give me some coordinates for the GPS, but he just kept laughing at me and said I needed to review the Navigation Chapter in my Private Pilot's Manual. He was right of course. We found Deep Woods without too much trouble and landed after a few obligatory low passes to check the condition of the runway.

Nothing can match a good party out at the airport with your airplane safely tied down a safe distance from the bonfire and good friends to help you keep an eye on her. We were the only 195 (thanks to Aubie's job and Jim and Val's schedule) and as usual she attracts a lot of attention and I love to tell stories about her and show her off to anyone who is interested. It is especially gratifying to meet up with someone who has flown a 195 "way back when" and you can actually share the limelight between old 66R and someone else willing to part with an interesting experience.

I met two former Cessna 195 pilots on this trip and I would like to share with you a couple of their tales.

WOODY McKAY

I had heard the name Woody McKay back in the 60s or 70s through various tales about skydivers and parachute centers and we even met at the Casa Grande, Arizona, Parachute Center that I was operating in the 70s. Here in Deland, Florida, I had the privilege of being reintroduced to Woody over a pile of chicken wings and cold beers.

In the 70s, Woody's parachute center was in Darlington County Airport in South Carolina. Woody also operated his crop spraying business and flew everything from cut-back Cubs, Piper Pawnees, and Stearmans. He flew sprayers for 12 years so that does attest to his piloting skills since he is still alive to tell stories today. Woody sold the spray business after being elected to the South Carolina State Legislature as a state senator where he served for several years starting in 1979. Also during that time Woody was the president of the Darlington National Speedway and officiated over the NASCAR events for 15 years.

Woody needed a good airplane for the skydivers so he leased a 1951 Cessna 195, N1096D, from Decimus Barbot of Florence, South Carolina. If you check the members section of the Cessna 195 website you will find that Desi still owns 96D today in 2008 (In fact, Charmian and I met Desi at the Crystal River fly-in this April. He told me that Woody was one of his best friends and if it hadn't been for him he would not have been able to have kept his 195 for so long).

Generating revenue from skydiving in the 1960s was not the easiest of endeavors, any source of income was welcomed by operators. Woody had sold a demo (demonstration jump in front of as large a crowd as possible) to the organizer of the annual Iris Festival at Sampler, South Carolina. He invited three of his most experienced regulars to participate in the jump and they, (Woody Benaker, Sherm Haulsin, and Bobby Farson, D- 911) all loaded into the 195 along with 17-year old Mike Barber to fly the demo. The weather was okay at Darlington but Woody knew that Sampler was prone to fog this time of year and since he had sprayed and flown around the area, he took the controls. Woody followed the main road to Sampler and the weather was deteriorating quickly as they neared the airport. He was down to 100 feet but knew the runway would be off the right side one half mile past the intersection he had just passed. Sure enough, he landed right on time.

As he taxied up to the Iris Festival the sponsor was delighted to see them, thinking there was no way he was going to see anyone land that morning. They were all fairly confident the fog would lift before the scheduled jump and relaxed around the office until it was time. This day, however, the fog proved to be a lot slower to lift. By jump time it was only up to 500 feet, way too low an altitude for the four jumpers. Normally the minimum altitude to open your parachute is 2,000 ft above the ground so they decide to reschedule the jump an hour later. After three hours it was apparent that the ceiling wasn't going to lift and

Woody walked over to the organizers and told them it was time to give up and asked if they would pay him enough money to cover his fuel expenses since he had at least shown up in good faith.

The organizers just laughed at him and stated flatly, "No jumpy, no payee!" After several futile attempts to reason with them, they said if they were to see a parachute in the sky, they would pay in full, otherwise "No jumpy, no payee!" Woody gave up and walked disgustedly back to the plane. He kept looking up at the clouds and the closer he got to the airplane the more angry he became and he decided he was not going to let these "Wuffoes" off the hook. He explained the situation to his jumpers and told them to stay on the ground while he was going to do a clear and pull from as high as Mike could get the plane.

He briefed Mike to climb as high as he could and still see the ground. On jump run he was to firewall the throttle and get the 195 going as fast as it would go. They even planned to enter the clouds momentarily then dive over the airport on jump run to gather up as much speed as possible. Woody put his gear on and as he crawled into the cabin he saw his three buddies right behind him with their gear on and ready to go. Young Mike did exactly what he was told to do and over the jump spot Woody crouched in the door, grabbed his ripcord, and dove headfirst into the slip stream. He said it was one of the fastest parachute openings he'd ever experienced, the Para-Commander snapped open behind him. He looked at the 195 between his feet only 50 feet above him and the other jumpers diving out of the airplane with ripcords in hand and parachutes streaming from their packs. All of the parachutes opened cleanly and everyone landed safely. Woody stomped over to the organizers and collected his full pay and left the airport in a rush, vowing to never do business with these shysters in the future.

In the normal course of running a parachute center, it is usually necessary for the management to be as dedicated to the sport as much as he is to aviation. As owner, you constantly agonize over the urge to jump with friends and customers and what needs to be done about flying the airplanes as safely as possible. I used to go for months without jumping and do nothing but fly the planes, then, out of nowhere a competent pilot would show up and you were free to jump as much as you wanted until the new pilot was burned out and he would disappear.

Woody had found Murice Coleman to be a good friend and jumper and also a talented Cessna 195 jump pilot willing to share the duties of flying on weekends. Mace, as Murice was called, was an engineer for the Forest Department and in May of 1967 he was flying a load in N1096D. Woody was crammed in the back of the cabin. He would be jumping behind four other jumpers. They were climbing to 7,500 feet for a 30-second freefall before they would open their parachutes at 2,000 feet. At 6,000 feet in the climb is where the trouble began. Mace turned around and yelled at Woody, "Woody, something's happening to me!"

Woody didn't understand at first and yelled back, "What?" Mace started to say it again but Woody watched in horror as Mace's eyes started to flutter and then rolled to the back of his head. Mace slumped over the control column, pushing it forward and the 195 nosed toward the ground.

Jumpers are naturally suspicious of jump planes and when anything unexpected happens they are on a hair trigger to exit. Why? Well, mostly because they can. Woody started yelling for them to get out of the way and it took only a second for the four jumpers ahead of him to get out. Woody says he was intent on exiting the plane himself but at the last minute he decided to check if he could help his friend.

Mace had an emergency parachute on as required by FAR when flying jumpers and at first Woody considered just releasing his seatbelt and throwing him out while holding onto the ripcord.

Mace would survive the fall but that wouldn't be much help for his unconscious friend. While pulling himself toward the door Woody grabbed Mace's shoulder and pulled him upright, the 195 immediately responded to the release of the weight on the control yoke and started to level out.

That's when Woody realized there may be some hope to save both Mace and the airplane. He then positioned himself between Mace and the door and wrapped a seatbelt around his own arm so he wouldn't have to worry about slipping out of the airplane. With one hand, he reached to release Mace's seat belt but as soon as he tried, Mace slumped back onto the yoke and the 195 would start down again. It took a couple of attempts, but finally the seatbelt came loose. Woody carefully began moving Mace out of the seat and clear of the yoke. He would alternate with his free hand from moving Mace around and grabbing the control yoke to keep the 195 level. Woody had to back partially out of the door, feet dangling in midair to get his stricken friend from the seat to the floor, all while flying the plane and attempting to maneuver Mace to the rear of the cabin. It took several tries, but he finally got this accomplished, including wrapping a rear seat belt around Mace to secure him in place. He then crawled into the pilot's seat and took control of the airplane. During the descent he dialed in Florence Flight Service Station and asked them to send an ambulance and paramedics to Darlington Airport and collect his friend.

Mace was rushed to the hospital and he was diagnosed to have suffered a cerebral hemorrhage and was paralyzed on the right side of his body including his eye. He was in therapy for three years and because of his age and determination he was able to regain the use of his body and in a short time after that Mace was reissued a second-class medical from the FAA and was able to again fly.

MARK BORGHORST

Mark was also a jump pilot and skydiver from the 60s and 70s and he is still the senior pilot at the Deland Parachute Center. On Sunday, after the party, Charmian and I flew back to Deland to fuel up and get ready to fly back to Houston. As I was filling the 195 with 100LL, the Twin Otter jump plane taxied up to the fuel pumps as well. There is a fellow who services the jump planes and supervises the jumpers between loads and he talked to the pilot and then proceeded to add the agreed upon amount of jet fuel. The pilot turned out to be Mark and he made a B-line to the 195. He complimented us on the beauty of our plane and said he used to fly jumpers with one at the Zephyrhills drop zone near Tampa in the 70s. I finished topping off the right tank and measured out the Marvel Mystery oil while Mark proceeded to relate his most memorable experience to me.

Mark grew up in Minnesota and learned to fly there. His first job was as a jump pilot in Zephyrhills, Florida. He flew the jumpers in the Cessna 180 and Twin Beech and right seat in the DC-3. When a 195 showed up he paired up with another pilot to get his check out. When they sat down in the cockpit and realized there was only one control wheel, Mark told the check pilot he might as well get out because either he would be able to fly it or not and if not there would be nothing the check pilot could do about it. The check pilot simply undid his seat belt and as he got out said, "You're right, see you later." Mark had no trouble with the airplane and became a 195 pilot for the center after that.

One day, while flying right seat in the DC-3 an FAA examiner showed up on the drop zone and the owner asked him to give Mark a check ride. After the ride the examiner asked for Mark's log book and complimented him on his ability to fly a "three" but then said he couldn't give him his type after seeing he had only 800 hours as a pilot. The owner got into the conversation and insisted that if Mark could fly the plane, he deserved the type rating and asked the examiner to show him a regulation that stated 800 hours wasn't enough time. Mark got the type rating.

N4395N as she looks today.

The 195 was N4395N, the very airplane members Calvin and Valerie Arter restored in 2006. It had the firewall forward from a Howard DGA with the Pratt and Whitney 985 hanging out there and was an outstanding jump plane. Another of our members, Val Slocum, now an MD-11 captain, has several hundred hours flying this plane as well.

In 1978 Mark was flying 95N while the parachute center was conducting tests on parachutes. They had a 180 pound rubber dummy with the experimental parachute strapped to it and two other skydivers would throw it out the door for the test.

Mark realized they were having a tough time getting the dummy out the door so he kicked the rudder to make their job easier.

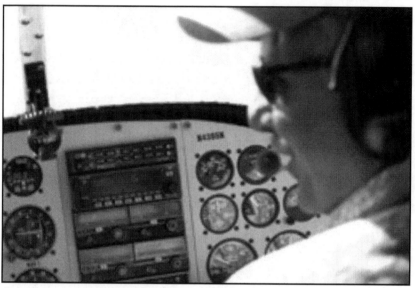

Cal Arter gracefully supervising Mike flying his carefully restored N4395N.

This time, however, the casting that holds the vertical stabilizer to the fuselage snapped and the stabilizer flopped over about 10 or 15 degrees. It wasn't tipped over very far but it was enough to jam the rudder push rod against the toilet seat bulkhead and the aircraft started to turn uncontrollably to the left. Mark added almost full right aileron and pushed the right rudder with both feet trying to keep the airplane on heading but it still kept turning slowly to the left. He had good elevator control and was able to make the 195 climb and controlled the left turn to five or six degrees per second. After gaining a little altitude, it was safe for the crew to exit the airplane. Mark briefed them to call for an ambulance and have it waiting for him when he attempted to land the airplane and if a crash occurred, they needed to get him out of the plane before it caught fire. Off they went and they notified the authorities of the emergency as soon as they landed.

Mark began a slow, careful descent toward the end of the runway. He was trying to time the turn so that he would arrive over the runway on heading and at a low enough altitude to land while close to runway heading. In fact, his first attempt got him to the ideal altitude but the airplane continued turning before he could land and after passing about 30 degrees off heading, he elected to go around and try again. He did better on the second approach and everything came together at the right altitude, heading and speed, he touched down close to runway heading and used the brakes for directional control and came to a stop without further problems.

When I think of the skill it takes to accomplish what Mark did, I marvel at his ingenuity and courage. Nobody knows what one would do in such a situation until it's their turn and you have to rely on your experience and skill to get you down safely. Mark had an emergency parachute and was an experienced skydiver so he knew how to use it. When evaluating his situation, I can only guess that having sufficient elevator control was the only reason he elected to try to save the aircraft.

Charmian and I said our goodbyes to our Florida friends and headed back across the complicated Florida airspace and spent another night with the folks at Shade Tree Airport in Mississippi. The next morning's flight was routine. It is always good to get home with another mission accomplished in the Cessna 195 without any hint of a problem from the airplane or the authorities along the way.

When you fly around in such a fine airplane you are bound to meet many fine new friends and always hear a story or two about someone's adventures while flying a Cessna 195.

12

OIL LEAKS

Shortly after Hurricane Katrina blew through the Gulf Coast, Charmian and I were asked to fly the 195 to Houma, Louisiana, to pick up the director of the Texas EquiSearch organization, Tim Miller. He had been working in New Orleans for the last five days and was exhausted and needed to return home for some rest. He would then fly to Phoenix to give a speech about his efforts in Aruba and New Orleans.

After arriving in Houma I was surprised to find a streak of oil coming from the left side of the cowling all the way to the tail wheel. Our engine is exceptionally clean running, very little oil is ever on the bottom of the fuselage. Rarely does it run past the second or third panel and that's without a clean kit. I cleaned the side as best I could with the rags and mineral spirits we always carry with us. It took two quarts of Aeroshell 100 to bring the quantity back up to four -and-one-half gallons, which is where we started when we left Hooks Airport in Houston. I made the decision to fly the plane back on that basis and we saddled up. By the way, there was no visible damage in Houma from Hurricane Katrina. They had power; everyone was smiling and the airport clean. The stories we heard from Tim over the intercom about the situation in New Orleans were quite alarming, but short in the telling. Our passenger was sound asleep within 15 minutes of takeoff. It was a pleasant flight to Bay Town just southeast of Houston where we dropped Tim and, once again I added two quarts of oil and departed for a 20-minute hop home.

Cessna N8266R flying along the Intercostal Waterway on way to Houma, Louisiana.

The next morning I removed the cowling and cleaned the engine and fuselage to try to determine what was leaking. The leak was located behind the cylinders. The front of the engine had remained clean and all of the oil was on the lower left side. There was oil residue burned on top of the exhaust bayonet. The firewall was covered with a thin coat of oil and the carburetor heat muff had oil running down the side and onto the ground. I had removed the oil cooler two years ago and resealed the regulator on top and that had cured a major leak at the time so I knew that was not the source. I tightened every connection, checked the oil filter, and tightened it. Then I started up the engine and discovered there was still a major leak somewhere. Next, I replaced the oil supply line to the oil cooler, cleaned everything up and did another run up.

The Jacob's engine which swings out from the Cessna 195 firewall for maintenance.

This time I ran the engine for only four minutes hoping that the oil would not spread so much and I could see where the source would be. No luck, there wasn't nearly as much oil but the source of the leak was just not discernible. The next morning I re-cowled the engine and we flew about 80 miles to a little Stearman fly-in south of Houston. I brought along plenty of rags, mineral spirits, and oil, but the leak, although still there, didn't seem as bad as before. I thought I might have made some progress but there might be one or two small oil leaks remaining.

I had to leave on a four-day trip for my job. On my return, I knew I would have one day to research the last of the oil leaks before we would leave for Saratoga Springs, New York, and the International Cessna 195 Convention. This year it was hosted by Bill and Jeanne Milton and Ken Sherwood at the Cessna 195 Factory, Saratoga Springs, New York.

September in Houston is always a nice time to work outside. This day the temperature would almost reach 100° F and it felt like the humidity was well over 120 percent. I pulled the cowling off and began cleaning the engine on the ramp in front of the hangar. I looked everything over carefully and started the engine for a few minutes. There was still a leak somewhere, but I just couldn't isolate it. I repeated the process two more times and there was still no obvious cause. This begins to get frustrating and I was beginning to lose my cool. In desperation, I removed the oil cooler and checked the work I had done two years ago. Everything was tight and nothing was obviously wrong. I replaced everything for the final run up; you can only work so long in that heat. Still, there was oil coming from somewhere, but I had run out of patience. I decided I would take an extra case of oil to New York and just live with a dirty airplane at the convention.

Our plans for the trip included a night in Pontotoc, Mississippi with Aubie and Leslie Pearman. Aubie had arranged a gourmet eight course dinner at a private residence not far from Pontotoc. We left Hook's Airport at 1:00 p.m. and decided to stop in Monroe, Louisiana (MLU), after only two hours of flying for the cheap gas. I really wanted to check the oil level.

It was gorgeous flight to MLU and we taxied to the south corner of the airport for the self-service pump. Two attendants met us at the pumps and as they walked around the 195 shaking their heads in wonder, Charmian and I felt a sense of pride in the time and effort we expend keeping this beauty the way she is. That was before I spotted the oil running out the left side of the cowling and all the way back to the tail wheel. I was very disappointed. It was exactly the same as it was in Houma and I had spent several days work for nothing.

I called Aubie to tell him the bad news and see if he had any suggestions. He did. He suggested we fly to Tupelo, 15 miles east of Pontotoc, and he would have his best mechanic, Clay, on it at six a.m. the next day. I thought that was a good idea. Obviously I wasn't able to fix the problem, so, even though I have the required mechanics ratings for this stuff, I'm really just a pilot and any tough mechanical jobs on our plane usually requires a professional.

I added another half gallon of 100 weight and we left for the one-and-one-half hour ride to Tupelo. When we arrived, Aubie parked us in front of his maintenance hangar and we were glad to see our old friend again. We cleaned off the side of 66R, pushed her in the hangar and headed to dinner. We were joined by Mark Kellum and his wife Joy and the six of us enjoyed a professionally prepared meal of giant proportions and excellent quality while we watched a Jet Blue Airbus make an emergency landing in LAX on the news.

Aubie was up at 5:30 the next morning and we headed back to the Tupelo Airport and some coffee. Clay was already in the hangar ready to pull the cowl off of 66R and fix my leak. I had seen Clay in action on several occasions here in Pontotoc and at Sun-n-Fun when the Lodestar needed a new magneto before they could leave, I knew we were in good hands.

We washed the engine and ran it up for a few minutes then inspected the area on the lower left side. It was the same as the other day and the first question was about the oil cooler, but I assured them that I had replaced the seal on the regulator and checked the cooler out the day before. Clay shook his head; my hopes that he would quickly see something I had missed were dashed. The one thing we couldn't understand was why the oil was literally streaming out of the carburetor heat baffling.

Immediately, Clay started unscrewing the clamps and removed the muffs, but still nothing obvious revealed itself. Clay washed the area again, and then instructed me to run the engine while he kneeled down next to the left gear to observe the area and see what was going on. With the carburetor heat muff removed he had an unobstructed view of the oil cooler and the carburetor. This time as soon as the oil pressure raised I saw Clay shake his head and signal for me to cut the engine. As the prop swung to a stop, he said through the open window, "You've got oil running out of the cooler. There must be a pinhole leak somewhere inside."

It was a relief to finally know that we had found the cause and I felt sure that with all of the 195 and Jacob engines around here, Aubie would have a spare oil cooler somewhere. It took about 15 minutes to change coolers and run up the engine. Everything was clean after the run up and we cowled the engine and taxied to the front of the Tupelo Aero hangar for a top-off. A few hours later the girls showed up and we headed northeast to Saratoga Springs!

At cruise altitude in a loose formation with Aubie, I thought over what had just happened. Why had I been so reluctant to blame the cause of that leak on the oil cooler? Now it seems so obvious, the first thing Clay and Aubie asked me about was the oil cooler. It was even one of the first things I had thought about when we came back from Houma, but I had quickly discounted that as the cause simply because I had worked on it two years prior. I couldn't admit to myself that it was leaking again. I have a spare oil cooler sitting on the shelf in the hangar and I could have avoided all that time and effort if I just hadn't had the preconceived notion that the cooler wasn't the problem.

Maybe that's the difference between a professional mechanic and a part-timer, or a mechanic and an aircraft owner. The professional mechanic can approach the airplane with an objectivity that the owner may not have. Whatever the difference, I learned that sometimes I have to step back from my beautiful airplane and make sure that the decisions I'm making about the care and maintenance are not tainted by my personal desire to save money, time, or preconceived opinions about previous work I might have done. For one reason or another, I was not capable of making the logical decision that Clay made. He walked up to a strange airplane having no previous experience with its history and quickly diagnosed the discrepancy after only a 15 minute effort, while I spent three miserable days diagnosing everything but the actual defect because of my previous knowledge of what had been done to the engine.

Okay, that's one more experience to put under my belt!

Mike and Charmian enjoying another flight in their 1949 Cessna 195.

13

YOU MEET THE NICEST
PEOPLE IN A 195

I've often thought I am the luckiest man alive. I am married to a beautiful girl who loves airplanes and is willing to live in our airplane hangar on a busy airport, I have a beautiful Cessna 195 that resides at the bottom of the stairs from our front door and, I live in a country that I can fly that airplane almost anywhere and anytime I chose. Since I have retired (2006), Charmian and I have flown over a hundred hours around the country exercising the privileges of American life to its fullest. Retirement is great, as long as the money lasts but, I'll worry about that later. I had the good fortune to read this bumper sticker soon after I retired.

A Fool and His Money are soon PARTYING

Since the 2005 Cessna 195 Fly-in at Saratoga, New York, Charmian and I had been planning an elaborate 195 trip for the following year during the 195 fly-in for 2006. The plans for this trip began to take shape after the phone conference when the 195 Club Board of Directors decided to move the fly-in up a week so some members could integrate the Reno Air Race into their plans. The 195 fly-in was now one week after the air races. That made perfect sense to me and we immediately started planning to attend the races. Several of the Cessna 195 Club members also committed to attend the races and we knew this was going to be a good year.

A month before the flight was to commence I read about the National Aviation Heritage Invitational sponsoring several aircraft to be displayed at the Reno Stead airport during the Air Race. I immediately sent them an e-mail and volunteered our Cessna. They accepted our offer and that meant we would have to fly into Stead early in the week and park in the Heritage area. Since aircraft not flying in the races were not allowed into Stead during the event, this would save us having to park at one of the surrounding airports and finding transportation to and from the race every day.

We arrived Tuesday evening and were welcomed to the show by several volunteers and parked in a temporary spot close to the fuel pumps. The volunteers helped us sort out the details of our transportation needs and handling instructions for the airplane and soon wanted to move the Cessna to the display area for the following week. I'm a little particular how our airplane is handled because of the polished aluminum that Charmian works so hard on, but my concerns were put to rest when I watched each volunteer don new white gloves before they approached our beauty. They moved the old girl up to the line, tied her down while a van full of snacks pulled up to take us to the hotel.

Wednesday morning our ride, provided by the Invitational, delivered us back to Stead and we were treated to breakfast and given our free entry passes for the rest of the week. We spent the morning cleaning 66R and completing the final touches for the display while several more show planes taxied up before the day's race events started.

Cessna 195 on display at the Reno Air Races. This display is sponsored by the National Aviation Heritage Invitational (2006).

It was a wonderful week of airplanes, friends and camaraderie. The days passed displaying our 195, wandering around the flight line and pit area, and partying with our 195 friends in the boxes on the flight line that Coyle Schwab had arranged for the Club. All of this time I kept thinking, *this is just the first week of our trip!*

Friday afternoon Charmian and I were walking behind the grandstands heading from the airplane to the box seats for a little break from the crowd. About half way to the box seats someone taped me on the shoulder and said, "Excuse me, is that your Cessna 195 back there at the Heritage show?"

I'm not shy about admitting to that and I turned around to meet a wonderful gentleman by the name of Harold

Wenzelburger from Paso Robles, California. He was up for the Air Show as he has done every year since Reno started and wanted to talk about the Cessna.

P-51 Mustang barrel roll at Reno.

We moved to the side of the path and Harold explained that he was in the Air Force from 1948 to 1952 and had been stationed at Ladd AFB, outside of Fairbanks, Alaska, as an aviation mechanic. He had wanted to fly in the Air Force but his eye sight had not met the requirements and chose the next best job he could think of. He was assigned to maintain C-47s and C-54s but soon heard about an opening at the air Rescue Unit across the field. He volunteered and was selected to join the unit. That's where he was introduced to the 3 LC-126s used in the searches over the Alaskan wilderness.

HAROLD WENZELBERGER'S STORY

For the next six months Harold helped maintain the Cessnas and flew on the search and rescue missions. The Cessnas were based in Fairbanks and Anchorage and there was a base in Adak for refueling and service but no aircraft. The Cessna LC-126s were mostly used for the local searches and the C-47s and C-54s for the long range missions. He said the pilots and mechanics loved the 126 for its reliability and ruggedness. Even the coldest of winter nights would not prevent the Cessna from participating in a search and rescue. When the need arose, Harold said the whole of Alaska Territory would rally to find a lost airplane. If it was near the Canadian border the Canadian Air Force would send its de Havilland Beavers to help out.

Harold Wenzelberger

Typically, the LC-126 was used mostly for searching for downed aircraft or lost personnel. The Air Force learned early on that back country landings on rugged terrain was not the best use of this asset. They would use all of the aircraft available to find a lost party and then send the para-rescue teams in to recover the survivors. The rescue team would load up in the C-54 with their dogs and dog sleds and all would parachute out as close to their target as possible. From there they would load up what they could and proceed to a location where they could be recovered. Sometimes this would be a strip suitable for the C-47 or a helicopter. Once, Harold knew of a para-rescue team that had to cut down enough trees for a helicopter to land for the rescue, at night! It's hard to believe, but Harold told me that the dogs had to be tied up in the airplane as soon as they boarded because they were so eager to jump out. Now, judging from the way our Doberman, Stormy, acts in our 195 I'm not so sure if they were as eager to go parachuting as they were to just get the heck out of the airplane. Imagine what went through those dogs' minds when they finally got to exit the airplane and found themselves hanging from a parachute a thousand feet above the Alaskan wilderness.

USAF Cessna LC-126 on floats stationed at Ladd Air Force Base, Fairbanks, Alaska.

Maintenance on the LC-126s was performed every 25, 50, 75 and 100 hours. Very little would go wrong with the Cessnas between the inspections and that was one of the reasons the Air Force loved the airplane so much. While Harold was stationed at Ladd they did lose one airplane which they were unable to recover in a landing accident in the back country. There was also a ground loop incident at Ladd and they were able to repair that aircraft and return it to service. In May they would put one airplane on floats and a couple of weeks later the second. Of course, in the winter the LCs would have skis installed.

LC-126 being lifted by crane to fit floats on for the summer.

When the aircraft first arrived in Alaska they found the Southwind heaters were not up to the job and there always seemed to be some problem with them. The Southwind Company sent a representative to Alaska to troubleshoot the unit and they worked for months to get the problem resolved. Most of the trouble seemed to occur in extremely cold weather; they found the heater was just not up to the task. Eventually the heater was redesigned in the lower 48 and the modifications sent to Alaska. They seemed to work satisfactorily after that. Harold stated that

Ladd was used as a testing and proving grounds for new equipment to see how it worked in the extreme conditions.

One day word came down about a new LC-126 in the states waiting to be ferried to Ladd for the unit. The plane was in Oklahoma at Tinker AFB undergoing modifications the Air Force felt were needed for use in the North.

The Air Force would fly the LC-126 with floats in the summer and skis in the winter.

One of the modifications consisted of replacing the rivets in the bottom the fuselage with larger, stronger rivets. Also, the heater was receiving its upgrade and when the plane was ready, orders were issued for Captain Roger C. Hammond and Sgt. Harold A. Wenzelburger to bring the plane to Alaska. Harold has been kind enough to send me the original order he received and it is as follows:

J. The folg named officer & airman, USAF, Flt "D", 10th Air Rescue Sq, ARS-MATS, Ladd AFB, Alaska, APO 731, US Army WP on TDY to OCAMA, Tinker AFB, Oklahoma City, Oklahoma for aprx fifteen (15) Days o/a 24 Oct 51 for purpose of picking up & ferrying LC-126 #49-1999 to this theater. DPUO. TBMAA. CIPAP. TC will furn trans. Commercial air (unreadable) from port of Aerial debarkation to Oklahoma City, Oklahoma as contributing to the more efficient accomplishment of the mission. (Joint Tvl Reg). Baggage not to exceed 65 lbs authd for tvl by mil acft, add 25 lbs authd per individual for tvl by (unreadable). Minimum clothing requirements prescribed by AAC ltr 67-18,26 May 50 will be complied with, Upon compl of TDY will ret to proper sta, TDN, 5723400 271-2300 P458 (.6)-os s65-501. Vou for reimbursement will be compl of tvl; paying office will forward paid copy to Budget & Fiscal Div 29th Depot WG, APO 942, US Army. Auth: AAC ltr 35-22, dtd 20 Mar 51; Msg (unreadable) 3-K-288, dtd 15 Oct 51.

CAPT. ROBERT C. HAMMOND A0540262
Sgt. HAROLD A. WENZELBURGER AF13298529
BY ORDER OF COLONEL ARNOLD

I can just imagine 21-year old Sgt. Wenzelburger's excitement when he received these orders. Even today flying the Alaska Highway is an adventure few of us lower 48 pilots will ever experience. When Harold talks about this flight you can hear the excitement in his animated voice even after 55 years have passed.

USAF LC-126 search and rescue mission over the Alaska wilderness.

Meanwhile back behind the grandstands at the Reno Air Races Harold, Charmian and I exchanged names, phone numbers and e-mail addresses. We agreed to get in phone contact to sort out a few more details and it is my honor to relate as much of this story to you as I can. Harold sent to me, along with his orders, an itinerary of his and Capt. Hammond's adventure and pictures he had taken at Ladd AFB. Incidentally, Harold's opinion of this fine aircraft is matched only by his high regard of the pilots who flew them. The conditions which these airmen were required to fly are the most demanding in the world and during Harold's tenure at Ladd AFB the loss of only one airplane is remarkable. Even better than that however, is not one crew member was lost or seriously injured while operating in this environment in the LC-126 during Harold's tour.

Here is the itinerary sent to Harold by Sgt. Wenzelburger:

THE FLIGHT USAF LC-126 #49-1999
From Tinker AFB, Oklahoma City, OK to
Ladd AFB Fairbanks, AK
Capt. Robert C. Hammond - Sgt. Harold A Wenzelburger
28 Oct - 21 Nov 1951

Dpt Tinker Field 11/6/51 at 1500 hrs. Arrive at the Cessna Aircraft Company 16:15 hr Cessna checked the modifications and we also had a chance to fly a 195 with cross wind gear that they were working on at the time.

Dpt Wichita 11/9/51 at 10:30-Arrive Lowry AFB, Denver at 14:00.

Dpt Lowry AFB 11/11/51 09:30. Arrive Casper, WY 11:30. Due to very high winds we had to make several landing approaches and finally two men came out to attach ropes to the wing tiedowns and I jumped out and laid over the rear of the aircraft to keep us on the ground. Under those conditions we got a hangar.

Dpt Casper, WY 11/11/51 09:45-arrive Great Falls AFB, MT 13:25

Dpt Great Falls AFB 11/16/51 10:45. Refuel at Lethbridge, Alberta, Canada -arrive at Edmonton RCAF Base 13:45

Dpt Edmonton 11/17/51 10:20. Refuel at Grande Prairie, Alberta-arrive Ft Nelson, British Columbia 15:20

Dpt Ft Nelson RCAF Base 11/18/51 09:00. After encountering icing conditions about 30 minutes into the flight we returned to Ft Nelson and were weathered in until 11/20/51.

Dpt Ft Nelson 11/20/51. Refuel at Smith River RCAF Base, BC and at Watson Lake, Yukon Territory-arrive at Whitehorse RCAF Base Yukon, Territory 13:40.

Dpt Whitehorse 11/21/51 19:45(?) (I think he meant 09:45-ED). Ran into whiteout and had to land at Eileson AFB, AK, a ten minute flight from Ladd, at 13:10. Weather finally broke and we departed Eileson at 14:30 arriving at Ladd AFB at 14:40.

Harold said, "Total flying time was 25:40 hrs including the short flight (1:15) due to icing problems out of Ft Nelson. Most of the delays during the flight were weather related. It was not the best time of the year to be ferrying a plane to AK.

"Hopefully after 55 years, at age 76, I have remembered most of the trip as it happened.

"All in all it was a great flight and one that I will never forget. The sights, all the people we met along the way, was probably my best memories of my 4 years in the USAF.

"Prior to our trip I was given basic instructions on takeoff and landings so that if a problem would occur with Capt. Hammond I would at least be able to get to a base along the way. I would say that it was lucky for both of us that nothing happened as I'm not too sure how I'd have done, but it was fun taking over the controls many times during the flight."

Indeed it must have been quite a trip for those two and thank you, Harold, for sharing your experience with us and thank you for your service to our country.

14

CESSNA SERVICE CLINIC
THE LAND DOWN UNDER

He flew his Cessna 195 into Wagga late on the first day of the Service Clinic making him the sixth and final aircraft to participate. David said hello to his friends and introduced himself to a few of the Americans who had travelled the 10,385 or so miles to help Craig Tabener make this event a reality. For the rest of the afternoon he quietly moved from airplane to airplane observing and learning, asking a few questions and listening intently to the answers. He wanted to know what was going to be done to his grand old Cessna 195 during the clinic and be able to apply what he was learning to keep it flying safely for another 70 odd years.

The sun closed in on the Australian western horizon and everything started to wind down as we began to close out our first day. At the Waga Aero Club across the parking lot, I tried to buy a beer but, odd thing about Australia; Americans don't seem to be able to buy their own beers over there. Before I could make my way to the head of the line at the bar, Rob Fox pressed a cold Carlton Draft Beer into my grateful hand. A Cessna 195 Service Clinic starts fairly early in the morning and continues on till near sunset but that doesn't mean everyone goes home. Like Oshkosh, half the fun is after the hangar doors are closed for the night and conversations about flying and maintaining our airplanes continues throughout the evening. Eventually our van driver announced it was time for departure so we packed up and headed for the hotel to freshen up for dinner. It was a short walk to the Victoria Hotel and a typical Australian Pub and soon we were once again socializing around a table with fresh libations and waiting for our various evening meals.

Typical clock found in Australia.

I had the very good fortune to be sitting next to David Friend, the afore mentioned late arrival earlier this afternoon. David has made a career ferrying aircraft around the world and I was astonished and amazed at the tales being told to me. What a remarkable career, what an incredible pilot to be able to successfully complete all of these flights over the most hostile environments possible. David's first job was in Alaska as a bush pilot, he found himself in Florida after deciding it was time to move on. He met a man desperate to have his Cessna delivered across the Pacific and David volunteered to complete the mission. Having never flown across the Pacific before, he assured the owner he had plenty of experience and he would leave as soon as the ferry tanks were installed. After that, finding jobs ferrying aircraft around the world seemed to come around and David did indeed become very experienced flying across the oceans.

On one occasion he found himself hundreds of miles west of San Francisco in a de Havilland Otter. The 600-hp Pratt and Whitney radial ground on endlessly as he flew beyond radio range for a position report. Oakland Center asked a United DC-8 flying along his route to contact the Otter and relay his position. This was a common practice so David had been expecting the call. After the relay, the United pilot asked "By the way, what kind of aircraft are you flying?" David explained what a DH Otter was and inquired if they had ever heard of one before, it is a fairly rare type of airplane. The UA pilot admitted he had never heard of an Otter, wished David a safe flight and signed off.

David flew on through the night, a couple of hours after sunrise, another UA DC-8 pilot called asking to relay his position to Honolulu Center. David gave the report and the airline pilot relayed it to Center then he also asked, "What are you flying?" Again David answered and again asked if they had ever heard of this rare aircraft. The UA pilot confidently answered, "Of course we know all about de Havilland Otters but they really can't be such a rare aircraft." He went on to explain, "Only yesterday we relayed a position report for another Otter pilot just out of San Francisco." David thanked the UA pilot for the relay and for the rest of the flight to Honolulu wondered if the other pilot ever realized he was talking to the same aircraft. We enjoyed a good chuckle about this and other fantastic tales coming from this remarkable gentleman. I wish I could remember them all to relay to you but this is a story about our Service Clinic so I'll press on.

OUR HOST FOR THE CLINIC

Charmian and I had arrived in Australia a few days early. We enjoyed an evening at Craig and Lara Tabener's house in Geelong, two hours south of Melbourne. Saturday Craig and I drove back to Melbourne to pick up Aubie and the rest of the Americans flying in for the clinic. What a treat to see these people in Australia, Aubie passed through customs first and a few minutes later Bill and Jeanne Milton walked out followed by Jeff and Anne Pearson. Craig had room at his house for one more person so Aubie came back to Geelong with us and Bill and Jeanne were collected by Mike Dalton and taken to his home, Jeff and Ann paired up with Rob Fox and stayed with him and his wife Catherine.

Our host Craig Tabiner made sure we were well taken care of throughout our adventure in Australia.

Craig had arranged to meet everyone at the Royal Australian Air Force Museum at RAAF base Point Cook (est. 1912) for a quick tour around that afternoon. Then we drove out to Little River, a farm with a private strip where Rob and co-owner keep the 195 VH-ONV. We were treated to a Barbie next to the hangar. During dinner we watched a refreshing aerobatic display by Darren Craven in his ex-RAAF Winjeel trainer We looked over Rob's airplane, conversed with our hosts John, Rob, and Catherine and finally headed back to Geelong (I love typing and saying that word {<u>GEEE</u> - long}).

The next day, Sunday, we would fly in Craig's Cessna 195 to Wagga Wagga where everyone would meet for the Clinic starting on Monday. Charmian and I had met Craig at Oshkosh last summer and that's where the idea to hold a Service Clinic in Australia was hatched. I offered to come early to help him organize the event. Craig told me he would be glad of the assistance but he had been the organizer of several events in the past and he thought we could just consult via phone or e-mail if any questions came up. That was a relief for me and Craig, with Aubie's help, did a fantastic job of making the arrangements, getting payment in advance, and making sure everyone could attend on the selected dates.

Craig grew up on a farm at Devenish, approximately 20 miles North of Benalla, Victoria. His father learned to fly when Craig was still young and they had a landing strip and hangar built on the farm when dad bought an Auster. Craig learned to fly at age 16. After his solo, he would fly the family airplane to the local airport for his flying lesson to prepare for his license. On one occasion he was delayed going home because his instructor spotted a CASA inspector (Australia's version our FAA) lurking around the airport. Craig's High School was 40 miles from the farm. Mum and Dad also worked in town so they would drive Craig and his brother to school. On occasion, when Dad was off and Mum couldn't make the drive, Craig would fly the family plane to town. He knew how to fly alright, but, he was still too young to have a driver's license. Dad eventually retired from his job, sold the farm, and became a full time flight instructor.

Auster

Craig and Laura Tabiner's wedding picture.

Craig and Lara met on a ski vacation and their first date back at home was going out to dinner. Of course it was in an airplane, flying to dinner. I asked Lara if that impressed her enough for her to consider a serious relationship? "Oh no!" she answered, her smile lighting up the room, "I'd already made that decision 10 minutes after we met on the ski trip. He'd already been had by then, he just didn't know it yet."

ON TO WAGGA WAGGA

Late Sunday morning Craig drove Aubie, Charmian and I to Lethbridge Airport where his Cessna 195 is kept. We pulled her out of the hangar with Craig's trusty HINOMOTO Best E14 tractor. The field was still quite muddy from the rains a couple of days previous and the 195 bogged down and stopped, buried up to its wheel pants. Craig pulled out tools, removed the pants, and towed her to a dry area where the line boy/flight instructor/general on duty does everything around the airport guy drove up with four 55-gallon drums of 100 octane. The fuel had to be hand pumped into the 195 and guess whose job it was to do that! Right, the line boy, flight instructor, duty to do everything guy. (A lot of us started our aviation career in the same way.)

We loaded up and began to back taxi down the grass runway. The old 195 was loaded to gross weight and I had some apprehension about the takeoff. Craig swung the tail around and as we headed down the runway, my concerns were soon forgotten when the 330-hp Jake reached full power and the 195 literally leaped off of the grass. I was used to our A-2 engine and we live at 5,000 ASL so it was a pleasant surprise. We headed north past Geelong, then Melbourne, and descended to just above the mountains to look for a way through the pass. Our first pass was a little obscured by clouds so Craig turned west where the hills were not so high and then we continued north.

Aubie Pearman driving Craigs tractor used to tow his Cessna 195.

Fueling the Cessna 195 Australian style. Look at the arm muscles on the Australian flight instructor/lineman while he pumps avgas from 55 gallon drums

In about an hour and a half we landed at the Brown Brothers Winery and Milawa Epicurean Centre for lunch. We were preceded by Mike Dalton and his passengers, Bill and Jeanne and a number of the Aussies' other friends in a collection of interesting aircraft. We waited for Rob Fox and Jeff and Anne but word came they would be delayed for a half hour so we ordered our meals. A half hour passed and we joked about Jeff must have seen Rob's airplane and offered to fix something before they left and he was still at it somewhere in Australia.

The Miliwa Epicurean Center, our stop for lunch.

In fact, that's kind of what happened. The 195's mag was acting up so they taxied back to the ramp and Jeff fixed it. In time they arrived and joined us for lunch.

Soon we were loading up again and heading to Whorouly International strip, only five minutes east. This is a beautifully maintained grass, one-way-in/one-way-out strip where owner Doug Hamilton keeps his stable of interesting airplanes. Upon exiting the airplane and introducing ourselves to Dougie, he took one look at Aubie and said, "Heck, I know you!"

A bunch of ravenous Australians and Americans.

Aubie looked him up and down and with his usual smile he answered, "Yeah! Well I bet you never expected to see me here, did you?" They are both Lockheed guys and had met at the Reno Air Races two years previous, Doug owns a beautiful L-12. We were shown around the hangar while Mike and Rob taxied up and introduced their American passengers. Doug and partner Lou had his Harvard preflighted and asked if he could fly part way to Wagga with us. Craig said of course it was alright then explained to us Doug was a member of the Southern Knights, a T-6 formation aerobatic team similar to our Aeroshell Team.

We continued on to Wagga in formation and Doug was doing rolls over the top of us when he wasn't hung on to someone's wing. The sun had just set when we landed so in short order the airplanes were tied down, unloaded, and the

Wagga Aeroclub invited us to their club house for a few brews and bull stories. No one was disappointed with the stories and soon we loaded into the van for our accommodations for the next few days. Rob had a house rented close to downtown Wagga and invited Charmian and I to stay in one of the rooms.

A stop at Whorouly International Airport.

THE INTERNATIONAL CESSNA 195 CLUB SERVICE CLINIC, DOWN UNDER

The next morning the van picked us up and we met the crowd back at the airport. Charmian and I were delighted to see long time club member Ken Patry from Toronto, Canada standing in the hangar waiting to perform his Gearhead duties. Ken called me a few days before we left Denver saying he and Georgina were going to try to attend the clinic. Aubie called everyone together and began to brief what we were trying to accomplish over the next few days and how we would go about it. He then handed out personalized Cessna 195 hats to each member attending. Now that was a nice touch and just about everyone wore their hats throughout the Clinic, not just us bald guys.

The final leg to Wagga Wagga.

The first victim, VH-KXR, belonging to Colin and Rhonda Taylor of Coonabarabran, Australia, was in the hangar and we set to work. Soon the cowling was off, the engine swung, the door posts open, and tail cone removed. Aubie, Jeff, and Bill swarmed over the airplane, showing Colin where many of the common areas of concern could be found, where he had to look to inspect for problems, and what should be done to insure the continued airworthiness of this fine airplane.

Before Colin's airplane was fully inspected, the gearheads set to work on Rob Fox's and Jon Clement's VH-ONV. Aubie was delighted to see this airplane flying in Australia. This had been his first Cessna 195. From Aubie, the airplane had been passed on to owners in Wyoming where they had added the bucking bronco symbol on the tail. Rob decided to keep the unruly bronco symbol since he thought his first few landings in the airplane resembled a bucking bronco and the symbol was appropriate.

Aubie conducting the morning briefing at the start of the Cessna 195
Service Clinic.

Cessna 195 gearheads awaiting their assignments during the Australian
service clinic. Ken Patry who flew in from Toronto, Canada conversing
with Tony Middleton's brother.

Somewhere between working on these first two airplanes I looked up and spotted Peter McDonald exiting from a taxi outside of the hangar. Peter and his family attended the 195 Convention in Frankfort, Kentucky, the year before and, though he just completed A-330 ground school, he was determined to help out with the clinic and learn what he could. We gave Peter a screwdriver and set him to work.

Jeff Pearson conducting service clinic on Jacobs engine with a bunch of interested Australian Cessna 195 owners.

WHAT ARE WE ACCOMPLISHING WITH THESE CLINICS

The Cessna 195 Service Clinic is the brain child of club vice president Aubie Pearman. Several years ago he opened up a discussion with the membership about organizing the Clinics using the Bonanza/Baron Society philosophy. Then club president Coyle Schwab enthusiastically approved the idea and gave Aubie the go ahead to organize the first clinics. Since then, we have completed five clinics (including Australia). It is not cheap for the club to hold these events. The experts who do the inspections have to be flown to the different locations, accommodations arranged, and some allowance for incidental expenses paid for. Even with the club charging the participants for either having their airplanes inspected or attending as a Gearhead, not all of the clinics have paid for themselves. I have seen the inspectors paying for their own meals and incurring personal expenses not covered by the fees charged to the participants. On a few occasions, the Club has covered any shortfall in the expense. Club President, Larry Nelson, has supported holding these clinics even if they are not meeting all expenses.

Re-assembling Michael Dalton's Cessna 195 after his turn in the barrel at the service clinic.

The benefit vs. cost overages is, in my opinion, enormous. Every member of the Cessna 195 Club benefits from the knowledge passed on and the improvements realized to our fleet. I can personally testify to the benefits of having Charmian's and my airplane subjected to one of these events was worth every penny, ten times every penny. I intend to have our Cessna 195 attend a Maintenance Clinic at least every couple of years. Additionally, I have learned as much about our airplane, and the fleet in general, simply by attending the Clinics as a Gearhead. The hands-on experience of helping to ready the airplane for its 'look over' is just as instructive as helping your mechanic ready your machine for its annual inspection.

I have asked the various participants to write down their thoughts from their perspectives. Larry has already expressed his thoughts in his edition of "Over the Numbers" at the start of the Newsletter. Here are the answers from those members who have responded.

Hi Mike,

My 2 bobs worth (Aussie slang for opinion, same as my 2 cents worth)

The local population of 195's has doubled since Craig and I imported ours back in 2010. We wanted classic family machines that were practical and comfortable but still the old style of machine we liked. The 195 was the perfect choice.

But we knew very little about them other than people's comments that they were "a bit of a challenge." Having made our purchases and arranged import, assembly, CofA etc we have since been on a learning curve in terms of how to fly them and how to maintain them - both without any significant local knowledge base.

So when the down under clinic was proposed by Craig it promised to fill a couple of gaps. Firstly in terms of our tech knowledge, secondly in respect of aircraft operation and finally in terms of plugging into the 195 network.

Initially I was mostly interested in the maintenance and flying perspectives. It was a given that I would enjoy the social side of things but as our 195 VH-VLD ("Scatterbolts") had recently emerged from extensive airframe rebuild work which saw her spend some months in a fuselage jig I was naturally keen to see what the experts thought of that. The biggest plus for me though was being able to fly with Bill Milton and have him find nothing fundamentally wrong with how I fly the old girl. Given we have pretty much had to teach ourselves how to fly them this was a big plus - I can't have been too bad as he let Jeane fly the last leg home with me while he was flying in something else!

As far as the network is concerned, I think we are well and truly connected now and have made some great friends in just a few days. Being on the other side of the world is sometimes a challenge for us particularly when shooting an email to someone we haven't met looking for advice or parts but the clinic has fixed that for us as well.

My sincere thanks to the 195 Club for supporting Craig's initiative on this event.

Michael Dalton

In my case with C190 recently imported from Florida, the Clinic was very beneficial as the aircraft is still in the assembly stage, and undertaking the Cessna SIDS program inspections has made the task very time consuming, but well worth the effort, as you know my aircraft was the only one with the lockable tail wheel supplied by the 195 Factory.

To have Bill Milton (the STC holder) sitting at the back of the aircraft checking the assembly and operation, was amazing.

I was very appreciative for the advice and comments by both Bill and Jeff Pearson, which will greatly assist me with the ongoing maintenance of the aircraft.

It was a pleasure for Suzanne and I to host our five guests in our home, and our 2 dogs Max and Rosco have only just recovered from Aubie and Jeff's ball throwing.

I hope the Ladies enjoyed the tour around the area with Suzanne, as she certainly enjoyed the company.

Tony Middleton

It may not be your problem, but check that your oil separator is correctly orientated. This is something I wouldn't have picked up had it not been for the recent 195 Service Clinic we held down under.

Craig Taberner

After the first day of the service clinic, the group discusses the finer nuances of flying Cessna 195s "down under".

15

2007 INTERNATIONAL CESSNA 195 FLY-IN

2007 International Cessna 195 Annual Fly-In
22 through 26 September, 2007
Wichita, Kansas

Charmian and I loaded up the old Cessna a couple of days early for our annual trek to the International Cessna 195 Club Fly-In this year in Wichita, Kansas. We had been looking forward to a Wichita fly-in for many years, I have a lot of past history in the city, and we still have relatives living and working in the Air Capital of the World.

We left Hook's Airport outside of Houston the Monday before the event to spend time with the family before the official start of the fly-in. We were rewarded with a 45-mph tail wind all of the way. In fact, old 66R was actually flying at speeds as fast as some of those old timers claimed a 195 would fly back in the 40s. The Garmin 496 started prompting us to begin our initial descent into Stearman Field (1K1), Benton, Kansas while we were still 46 miles south. As soon as I dropped the nose over a little, the ground speed registered 235 mph! I rechecked the

ASOS at Jabara Airport, about eight miles from 1K1, and I was a little concerned about the ground wind still reported as 22 gusting to 33 kts. Fortunately the runway at Benton was lined up right into the wind. We reported downwind at Benton, but everything was quiet around the airport. On final we started to pick up light turbulence. I carried a little extra speed on the long, slow final approach, and nothing unusual popped up so the landing was routine with the nice slow ground speed on touchdown.

I really wasn't surprised that we were the only 195 there that early in the week. I diligently worked the ailerons to keep the wind from blowing the wing up while taxiing northbound and found a good spot across from the gas pumps to tie down. Charmian, our dog Stormy, and I exited the airplane, then secured 66R with our Fly-Ties and wrapped the cowling in case of rain. We then waited for my cousin, Bill Hawks, to come around to pick us up.

While we waited, I took stock of what I could see of the airport. The 2,600 foot runway is almost new black top, well taken care of, clean. It has very few blemishes that I could see. There is a parallel turf runway on the west side of the paved runway that was mowed and trimmed and ready for the weekend festivities (although a little rough, I found the turf to be my preferred runway). Houses with hangars lined the west side of the airport and there were more hangars on the east. There are taxiways between the hangars on the east side leading to a residential area with several houses and hangars. Um, those are my kind of people. The north end of the runway is displaced slightly to compensate for the close proximity of the county road. On the northeast corner is a hangar and office next to the self serve gas pump where we found a secretary on duty. She kindly advised us that the airplane was just fine where we parked and we were in a good spot to stay for the weekend.

The next day was a wonderful family affair but I kept a close watch of the website for any comments from our 195 friends en route to Kansas. Coyle and Sue Schwab were making their way from the Chicago area and had the same strong winds we experienced coming up from Texas which unfortunately translated into a headwind for them. Coyle wrote a comment in Hangar Talk about only going 98 knots over the ground. He and Sue finally made it in later that evening but we were still picnicking with the family and didn't hook up with them until the next morning.

Wednesday proved to be a gorgeous clear day. The winds had subsided to around eight Knots from the south, right down the runway. We arrived at the Benton Airport a little after nine a.m. and found five or six additional Cessna 195's tied down. Stephanie and the whole Huckins family were manning the welcome tent. They were busy handing out goody bags full of trinkets and memorabilia for the event. Charmian and I picked up our treasures from Stephanie and walked over to the other airplanes that had arrived to meet and greet as many members as we could. Every now and then the familiar drone of a healthy Jacobs or Continental radial engine caught our attention and everyone would turn and watch a sparkling Cessna 195 fly over and enter the pattern. The touchdown zone was right behind our 195 and no one escaped the attention of the members already on the ground while they attempted to make the best landings of their lives. Some did and some did not, but the sight of the magnificent old airplanes touching down less than a couple of hundred feet in front of you is breathtaking, even if the landings were not all perfect. We all enjoyed the efforts made by the arriving pilots. Everyone knows this is a tough crowd to land in front of. That may have made the effort somewhat intimidating for some. Throughout the entire weekend, not one airplane encountered a mishap or suffered a single scratch on landing or takeoff that I know of!

We had lunch under the wing of our plane and soon the arrivals began in earnest. It seemed every couple of minutes or so another 195 would make a right turn onto final approach and land in front of us. We recognized a few of the airplanes, but there were a lot of them that I had never seen before. It was fun to walk over and meet new and old friends alike. Soon the welcome tent was surrounded by registrants looking for their paperwork and asking questions about the coming weekend. I don't know how Stephanie kept up with all of the folks vying for her attention and looking for answers but no one walked away without experiencing her infectious smile and enthusiasm.

I was watching the goings on at the tent when I recognized the familiar voice of Richard Pulley and Ina Vleeshouwer greeting Charmian as they walked up from their airplane. They had flown into Dallas from their home outside of Anchorage, Alaska, on the airline, then driven to Fredericksburg, Texas, and picked up 36A, Richard's 195, to fly it to Wichita. We spent a good half hour catching up on the last couple of months since Charmian and I had visited them in Alaska. Richard asked if one of the vans donated by Cessna Aircraft Company for member transportation could take him over to Mid-Continent Airport to pick up his rental car. I didn't think it would be much of a problem and briefly considered taking him and Ina over there in our borrowed car but I came to my senses immediately. Why would Charmian and I drive our good friends all the way over there when old 66R was sitting there, her nose pointed longingly up at the sky, just aching to go flying. It made sense to Richard and Ina as well and we hopped in and headed southwest for a quick flight across the Air Capital. We landed on 19L at ICT, I knew from the old days Yingling Aircraft was on our right so I told my friends to be ready and I would drop them off without shutting down the engine, we would then head back to Stearman Field. On the way in I dialed in clearance delivery and told them of our intentions and they gave us a new squawk and a clearance back out of the Class C airspace. We had only a short wait at the end of the runway and were cleared for takeoff. Departure cleared us direct to Stearman but kept us advised of the traffic in the pattern around Jabara Airport. It was a real treat. We flew over many of my old stomping grounds from when I was in High School here in Wichita back in the 60s. This is the first opportunity I have had to fly my airplane over the city since then. Now you may understand why I was so anxious to have a fly-in at Wichita.

Richard Pulley wheel landing his Cessna 195 at Benton, Kansas.

I told the controller we had Benton in sight and he pointed out traffic just north of the airport, probably in the pattern. I could see a red Cessna 195 approaching the airport at high speed, definitely not landing. I called him in sight and the controller cleared us off his frequency. Before we left for ICT, Coyle told us that Scott and Janet Hartwig would be arriving very soon so I thought the red airplane making a low pass was them. I keyed the microphone and said, "Hey Scott, is that you?"

Scott quickly answered affirmative and I asked if we could join up on his wing for the next pass.

He said, "Sure can, but we're still 35 miles northeast!" I took a closer look at the 195 over the airport and noticed it had a red and white checkerboard tail. There's only one 195 that I know of with that design, Calvin and Valerie Arter from Lakeland, Florida in their Pratt & Whitney powered Cessna 196. I told Scott he had better hurry up then informed Cal we were coming up on his right wing and would join up on him instead of Scott. Cal said he had us in sight but he was taking it easy on his demo since he had a VIP on board. VIP, what's he talking about? As we pulled into position, I could see who it was. Mort Brown was in the right seat looking over his shoulder and smiling at us as only a 99 year old former test pilot could smile. He was grinning from ear to ear and giving the thumbs up. I told Cal we would pull ahead and fly lead so Mort didn't have to turn so much to watch the action. We did a lazy left turn back around to the north and lined up on the runway again. I couldn't have been more proud to be flying our 195 in formation with Mort Brown. Mort Brown, the very man who was the first to fly our plane on her production test flight, the gentleman who had test flown over 850 Cessna 195s and logged over 20,000 hours before retiring from the Cessna Aircraft Company. We did one more pass then Cal called downwind for a full stop. I pulled out ahead while they slowed to approach speed and Scott called. He had us in sight and would join up on our right. We cranked the two 195s around the pattern for a few more minutes and landed. Well, the fun had begun, and this was just the first day.

Airplanes continued to arrive while we were flying to ICT with Richard and Ina so it took some time to catch up on who was there. Many people were starting to leave the airport for the hotel to get ready for the dinner at the *Scotch and Sirloin*.

Charmian and I were invited to dinner at the family farm just east of Benton so we didn't have to leave until just before sunset. We continued to watch the activity around the airport when an unmistakable drone of multiple Jacobs engines could be heard over the laughing and hollering around the registration tent. All eyes turned to the west as 3 Cessna 195s appeared in the pattern in a V formation. In the lead was the yellow nosed, olive drab LC-126 from Chino, California, flown by Jeff Pearson.

Formation flying on way to lunch at Beaumont, Kansas.

"The Californians are arriving," someone yelled from the crowd. The formation kept their speed up on base leg and turned final. Simultaneously all three airplanes lowered their noses toward the end of the runway, and the sound of the three Jakes reverberated across the airport. Jeff zoomed past first, followed by Roger Vanderwindt and Bill Curruthers from Phoenix, then Lloyd and Sharon Sorensen in the King of Iza from Santa Ynez, California. One by one they pulled up and re-entered the downwind pattern. Jeff made a low sweeping turn toward the runway and touched down in a shallow bank with barely a chirp from the right tire. As the airplane rolled out onto runway heading, the left tire and tail wheel touched down without a sound, a remarkable demonstration of airmanship. When Jeff parked on the grass next to us and was idling his engine prior to shut down, I walked up to his open window and shook his hand and told him, "That was the lousiest landing I have ever witnessed!" He tried to punch me through the window but someone showed him an adult beverage waiting, and he shut down the engine instead.

As the sun began to set and the crowd started heading to the hotel I couldn't help smiling while I went over the events of the day. In the words of our Club Founder, Dwight Ewing, "Something about it, but you hardly ever find a clinker flying a Cessna 195!"

Heading home after lunch.

VOLUNTEERS

Events on the scale of the International Cessna 195 Club requires a lot of help from volunteers. Last year the local EAA chapter showed up in force at Santa Ynez to make the fly-in run smoothly, and this year the volunteers were just as enthusiastic.

Arrivals lining up for landing after lunch.

Throughout the event there were several golf carts and four wheelers running up and down the flight line offering to transport the club members back and forth to their airplanes and the office or tent. There were several large vans available for transportation to the hotel or anywhere in Wichita a member may want to go. These vehicles were manned by various locals, from club member Rose Pelton to airport owners Greg Largen, Dwayne Clemens, Vic Reeth or other local pilots from the field. The three shuttle vans were driven by Barb and Phil (Geo) Giovanni, Bob Bradshaw (who did the 195 sketch rolled up in your welcoming bag), Jim Barackman, Bill "Geeves" Robbin, and Jess "Humph's" Humphreys. Some of the four wheelers towed portable fuel tanks up and down the flight, line and if your bird needed fuel, you merely raised your hand when one drove nearby. Someone would have your tanks serviced within minutes. Then there was the entire Huckins's family. The official event host was Marvin-Eddie and Stephanie Huckins but I didn't realize there were so many Huckins's in the whole world, let alone the number of them running around Stearman Airport looking for someone to help. The hours the volunteers worked lasted far beyond the time we spent at the airport. After most members were relaxing in their hotel rooms or the local restaurant/lounge, these volunteers were still busy meeting stragglers at the airport and helping address members questions or concerns at the hotel. Without them this event would not have been near the fun it was. The lack of any major disruptions (with the small exception of the BOMB SCARE on Sunday morning) proves their dedication was instrumental to making a successful event.

BEAUMONT

Pilot Getaways Magazine has several articles written about flying into the Beaumont Hotel for dinner. The Beaumont Hotel was only 30 miles from our fly-in this year making a fly-out to this famous hotel mandatory. It was scheduled for day two at 11:30 a.m. to 1:30 p.m. The sound of radial engines starting began right on time and soon the parade of 195s began to roll past the registration tent. One of the local Benton pilots just happened to be my cousin's/wife's/brother. With such a close relationship, Jim Ralston, Charmian and I became instant friends, and we invited Jim to fly with us to the Beaumont Hotel. Jim had done this flight many times before but never in a Cessna 195 and did not hesitate to accept. We usually have our puppy dog with us wherever we fly but she weighs in at 75 pounds, not large for a Doberman but she does take up her share of the backseat of a 195. We asked Coyle if we could leave her tied to his tie down so she could stay under the shade of his wing. Coyle was hanging around the airport helping Stephanie and greeting almost every new arrival so he said it would be no problem leaving her there. He would keep an eye on her.

Meanwhile, long time member Jerry Johnson was en route to Benton from his home in North Carolina. Jerry decided to stop in Parson, Kansas (90 miles east), since the headwinds were stronger than forecast, and he wanted to arrive at the fly-in with plenty of fuel. After topping off, he hopped back in his 195 but was unable to get the old Jake to fire up. After trying everything he could think of (after all, Jerry had been flying his beauty for 15 years) he gave up and reluctantly dialed Coyle's cell phone to give him the bad news. When Coyle's phone rang, as luck would have it, Jeff Pearson was standing nearby and when Jerry told his story, Coyle knew immediately whom they needed to consult in order to resolve the issue. Jeff spent several minutes on the phone going over the symptoms of the problems and making several suggestions on how it should be handled then wished Jerry good luck. The gaggle of 195s was steadily heading for Beaumont and Jeff decided to jump into his LC and join the fun.

We also taxied out in a line of three other aircraft and waited our turn for takeoff. Craig and Jessica Wollmershauser were in front of us and Marvin Eddie was behind. Marvin called on the radio and asked that Craig and I form up in formation after takeoff and he would get some pictures for the fly-in. We both agreed, and soon we were in a loose two-plane when Marvin flew up on our left with a video photographer. We tried various poses and positions until everyone had enough pictures then headed for the Beaumont airport. I personally had no idea where we were but Jim leaned up between the seats and pointed us in the right direction. We could see three 195s in various stages of their approaches to the 2,000 ft grass runway so we passed just south of the field and entered a left downwind. I tried to get a close look at the airport as we passed. One Cessna 195 had just landed and was taxiing off the south end of the runway onto the city street. Several other 195s had already taxied down the street and parked in the lot across from the Beaumont Hotel. This was going to be fun!!

On base I watched traffic ahead touchdown and roll out towards the south end. I lowered the flaps and began to slow the plane. A 2,000 ft runway is not a great challenge for a 195 as long as you don't get too far outside of a normal approach. I wanted the speed back to just below 80 mph over the fence, which took a considerable amount of effort to keep the nose up high enough that it almost blocks the view of the touchdown zone. Even after a thousand or so hours in 195s, I still have a tendency to lower the nose for a better view, and then the speed starts to pick up. I'm getting better at it though and my landing was on the north end of the touchdown zone and not bad even if I say so myself! I have to say so myself since there was no one there to watch and document it except Charmian and Jim, and I have trouble bribing either of them to tell the truth on a good day.

We added a little power to taxi up the hill and then back to idle and brakes to slow us down when we crested and started down to the city street. It was a smooth transition to the black top road, and I followed Craig and Jessica toward the hotel. There is a stop sign between the airport and the hotel and I didn't want to take a chance of getting a ticket so I stopped then continued on and we parked right outside of the hotel's front door. Since the tail was pointed at the sidewalk and there were a lot of people walking around, I shut the engine down immediately. I like to use the procedure of idling the engine for a few minutes after pulling the prop control out but not in a situation like this. There were just too many smiling friends walking around enjoying themselves.

It only took a few minutes to get in line for the buffet provided by the hotel/restaurant. The roast beef and mashed potatoes were good and disappeared from my plate quickly. There were a couple of new faces in the hotel as well. John and

Marilyn Collett had flown directly from Goodland, Kansas to Beaumont as well as our close neighbors Dave and Sue Cole from Conroe, Texas. We sat with Dave and Sue and then paid the bill and headed for the airplane. I had the idea that if we hurried back to Benton, we could be there to watch all of the arrivals.

It didn't turn out to be that good of an idea because as soon as we got to the airplane, Rob Stalford (Rob keeps his airplane in our hangar in Houston) walked up with a camera crew from the local Wichita television station KSN. He was talking to the guy with a microphone saying something like "Here's a good person to interview." I quickly looked around to see who he was talking about and check out any avenues of escape, but Charmian suddenly wrapped her arm around my waist and smiled brilliantly at the camera. You gotta know when to fold 'em, and I knew I was had at that point. I mumbled something about 195s and taxiing on a city street and the fact that I grew up in Wichita and suddenly we were done and pushing the airplane into the street to leave.

The stop sign was posted for eastbound traffic as well so I stopped and looked both ways for traffic then proceeded down the road toward the airport. What fun!

Meanwhile, back at Stearman Field, Stephanie, the Huckins family, and Coyle and Sue had everything under control as we taxied back to our tie down. We walked over to retrieve the old puppy, and she was smiling and wagging her long, curved tail as we approached. Coyle said she was calm and collected right up until we flew past on our low approach when we returned. As soon as we went by she jumped up and started wagging her tail and whining. How she knew it was us no one knows, but dogs do have a way with these things.

We settled into our lawn chairs behind 66R and watched the arrivals inbound from Beaumont. Jeff Pearson made the obligatory low pass and then another impressively suave landing, and I had to grumble about how it's not possible to do that every darn time. Jeff wasn't on the ground long before we noticed him taxiing out and he departed to the east. Turns out, as soon as he landed another call from Jerry Johnson came in, and he was still stuck in Parson trying to get his plane started. When Jeff figured out where Jerry was he palmed himself in the forehead and said he had been half way to Parson while he was in Beaumont and if he'd figured that out earlier he would have gone over from there. Oh well!

There is only one thing to do when a 195 is stranded. Jeff didn't give it a second thought about jumping back into his LC for a rescue mission. After arriving in Parson, it soon became apparent that the old WWII era coil had finally given up after 60 plus years of faithful service, and Jerry was going to need a new one. They reluctantly left the airplane there, and Jerry rode on to Benton with Jeff.

But the story doesn't end there! After arriving in Benton, the search for a coil began in earnest. They started at the registration desk, but Marvin knew only that John Collett had them in Goodland, Kansas and suggested that they track him down and see if he could have one shipped in. It took a few moments to find John and Marylyn's airplane and finally the whole story of woe was told. John listened carefully and at the end of the tale he smiled and began to explain what he would do. I can hear his slow Kansas accent now, "Well, I did just happen to bring a Butterfly Coil with me and I was planning on using it for a door prize Saturday night but I guess, as it turns out, you just won the door prize!" John reached into a box and handed the coil to a slack jawed Jerry who just didn't know what to say at that point.

Our dog Stormy waits patiently under the wing for us to return from lunch.

Jerry told me the next day after we toured the Cessna factory, he and Jeff started to comb the ICT airport vendors to see if they could find the necessary wires, connections, and clamps to install the new coil. They found some of the pieces at Bevan-Raball, and Tim in the office spent considerable time helping them track down the right wires. That helped but there were still several parts needed. They found out there was a 195 project belonging to Ben Sorenson. Jeff said it was like a scavenger hunt. They would go down the list one at a time and by late afternoon they had all of the parts, some from ICT and some from Ben's project. They promised to replace what they took before he would actually need them.

Saturday morning, after the maintenance meeting, Jeff and Jerry loaded up in the LC again and headed east to retrieve Jerry's airplane. It took only a couple of hours and the old girl started right up and they headed back to Benton with both airplanes in formation. Sounds easy doesn't it? Not quite as easy to do as it is to relay this story to you, but the fact that it happened is the real story.

Aviation is a tight community and when you narrow it down to specifics, like down to 195s it gets even tighter! Where else can you call your club's president and be handed off to one of the most knowledgeable members to troubleshoot a problem while you're out in the middle of the boondocks and expect that within a few hours that expert will be crawling up a ladder to find out what's wrong. Then to be handed the specific part you need with a simple, "Well, I guess you just won the door prize!" And have the members looking for everything else you need in the middle of a party and in a strange town for two days, just to get your airplane back in the air is more than you could expect from any aviation community, but here it is. It happened, and it happened at our fly-in!

OLD TIMERS

I mentioned before about flying formation with Calvin Arter while he had Mort Brown, the 99-year old Cessna chief production test pilot with him. One of the most exciting aspects of the build up to this fly-in was the rumor that Mort would be at the event and would be telling stories and signing autographs. There was another aspect that promised equal excitement, the Cessna Retired Employees Association was invited as well as the test pilots.

I had the privilege of spending an hour or so conversing with Slim Reddout who was the flight line supervisor at the Pawnee Plant south of Wichita close to the old Wichita Municipal Airport (This is where my Uncle Mac took me for my first airplane ride in a Cessna 190. I was five years old). Slim supervised the preparation of the new Cessnas for their first flights when they emerged from the production line. He had many stories about Mort Brown and Dwane Wallace from over the years and he wasn't shy about telling them to anyone who was lucky enough to be there. He had great admiration for Dwane and remembers a close relationship with his boss and fair treatment. Mort and Sharon Brown compiled a loose leaf binder with information and quotes from the retired Cessna employees, and it will be a valuable and treasured possession for everyone who received one. It is titled: "Cessna 190/195 Trail Blazers" and has several pictures of the Cessna employees in the 40s and 50s and articles on the history of Cessna in general and a few on the Cessna 195 series specifically. It is fascinating to read and review periodically and provides an insight into the development of general aviation in the 1950s.

Let me quote the letter written by Slim Reddout and included in the handout all attendees received from Mort and Sharon Brown.

190 - 195 Recollections
Written By: Warne Reddout
Production Flight Line Inspector at Cessna Aircraft

Warne recalled that they improved the 195 over the years. He said a lot of the people who owned 195s enjoyed them. He recalled that Dwane Wallace was selling 195s without engines. Cessna bought war surplus engines and then installed them. The government put the 300 Jacobs engines on the market for $300, and sold as war surplus. Dwane arranged to have the engines "pickled," which meant they were lying around four to five years. The engines would get into the Engine Build-Up Department, where they drained the "pickling" oil out of them, just like from the factory. The engines were the property of the customers. Cessna adapted them for the 195, adding the baffles, exhaust stacks, and other accessories. The Engine Build-Up

Department prepped the engine, added mounts, and mounted it to the airplane. The inspector over the Engine Build-Up Department had a hoist or a dolly to mount the engine. The normal process of building up the airplane allowed the customer to save several thousands of dollars. The airplane, if he recalled correctly, was $5000 from the factory, and the war surplus engine was $200 to $300. It allowed Cessna to sell a lot more airplanes. Dwane was on top of everything. If he could adapt airplanes to sell with war surplus engines, they did so, and had it certified through Engineering Test Flight.

During the time I talked to Slim, he related a few of the incidents that occurred on the flight line while he was working. He said they would go over everything on the airplane before they would release it for flight test, but every once in a while, no matter how conscientious you are, something will get through.

I had the privilege of knowing one of the production test pilots, William (Bill) McNeil, when I was growing up in Wichita. I met Bill on a hot July morning at the end of the runway at the Pawnee Plant where I had been watching the airplanes for several hours. Bill was testing an unpainted 210 and taxied off the end of the runway and shut down. He then walked over to the fence and offered to take me for a ride! That's a whole other story so I'll save it for later, but when I asked Slim if he knew Bill McNeil, his eyes lit up, and he couldn't say enough about the integrity and honesty of that man. I already knew that about Bill but it was good to hear it from someone else. Charmian and I had visited Bill McNeil's gravesite the day before, and it was good hearing Slim talk about my old friend and mentor. It was a very emotional moment for me.

One of the incidents on the flight line I remember Slim relating was about a 310 attempting to takeoff with the ailerons rigged backwards. Whenever this happens, the pilot is rarely able to analyze and adjust his control inputs in time to keep from crashing, and on this morning the aircraft, was destroyed. Fortunately, the pilot walked away. Slim said it took only a few moments before Dwane Wallace was on the scene. The pilot was able to describe what happened. Dwane seemed to realize the inherent risk in flying and knew these things were part of aviation. Although not happy about the loss of the 310, he did not blame the Line Inspectors for the mishap but put the responsibility squarely on the pilot who should have recognized the reversed controls before he took off. Dwane then took Slim off to the side, and he casually related to him a story about the time he had taken off in a single-engine aircraft on its first flight with the ailerons rigged backwards. He said it is a difficult situation, but he had been able to recognize the discrepancy and successfully flew the airplane around the pattern and landed without damage. Throughout our Cessna 195 Meet in Wichita this year, one of the things I heard most was that Dwane Wallace was not only a good leader of Cessna Aircraft Company, but (much like the current CEO of Cessna, Jack Pelton) he had the reputation of being an excellent pilot as well. He was instrumental in much of the experimental test flying during the 40s at Cessna, and he obviously knew how to build good airplanes.

When you flew into Benton, Kansas, in your Cessna 195 this year and reached the tent where you picked up your packet from Stephanie, you were then introduced to Sharon Brown (Mort Brown's beautiful and energetic wife). Sharon would then introduce you to Mort, and just in case you didn't know who he was, she would explain that Mort probably was the first person to ever fly your 195 since he test flew over 850 on their first flights. Once she had your attention, Sharon would then hand you either the loose leaf binder that she and Mort put together or a DVD copy, whichever you preferred. If by chance Mort was not at that moment engaged with other 195 enthusiasts, you were allowed to ask any questions you liked. More than likely, however, throughout the weekend, Mort and Sharon were swarmed with people interested in what this gentleman had to say. As I said before, Mort is 99-years young, but you wouldn't guess it when you met him. He is a spry, slender man who gets around alright and when you talk to him, his mind is as sharp as they come. Mort and Sharon were at the airport every day and they appeared to enjoy themselves immensely. Every time I noticed them they were surrounded by 195 people with cameras and questions at hand. Mort spent hours with our members and I could only hope that what was passed on from this remarkable man can be documented by our club. Sharon is doing a valiant job of trying to save the history of Mort's career, and we all applaud her effort and hope to see more of her work in the future.

There is one more item from the handout prepared by Mort and Sharon Brown I'd like to bring to your attention before I close this chapter. Towards the back of the binder is an article written for the Cessquire newsletter published by Cessna for their employees. The article is titled: 195 Fly-In At Wichita. I am assuming it was written in 1970 after the first 195 Fly-in which was indeed held in Wichita. There is a quote in the article from an old timer who was instrumental in not only promoting the Cessna 195 but is also the founder and, for many years, the president of our club. I submit to you the words spoken by Dwight Ewing from that publication:

"We felt we should band together to maintain the skill required to fly and maintain the airplane. We have airline pilots, doctors, lawyers, businessmen, men with great social grace, some with none. But all are human people and all admire the 195s integrity as a machine. It has its faults, but it isn't sneaky about them."

Ewing continued: "It is a classic design, with its cantilever wing, an excellent fuel system and an electrical system that is simple but beautifully designed. Everything fits together into a good airplane."

AMEN DWIGHT

I have spoken with Dwight several times over the last year, and he was looking forward to joining us in Wichita but at the last minute he felt it would be unwise to leave Veta, Dwight's ailing wife, for such a long period. Dwight has said that they originally planned to return to Wichita for the annual meet every ten years but it just hasn't turned out that way. Why not? Well, there has been no shortage of interesting locations and capable members willing to host the 195 meet over the years, and I think it just fell by the wayside. I don't believe that will happen again after the time we had this year. My only comment about that is why not go to Wichita more often than every 10 years, how about five years or three years?

Club Founder Dwight Ewing with 99 year old Mort Brown.

16

WHO KNEW MY MOM?

The Cessna 195 website is one of the most valuable assets a Cessna 195 owner has to learn about maintaining, flying, or just enjoying his airplane. There are millions upon millions of websites available about almost any subject and I am able to keep up with only a few that I am really interested in. The 195 site is naturally at the top of my list, 4 or 5 times a day usually!

It was quite a surprise when an old skydiving friend from the 1970s sent me an e-mail about a post on one of the many skydiving sites he keeps up with (dropzone.com). The post was from a 30 year old woman. It read as follows:

> **Seeking skydivers who knew my mom**
> *My mom Carolyn Reynolds was killed skydiving on March 27, 1970 in Jefferson County, Colorado. She was 28 years old. She was with friends/skydivers Charmian Cliff, Joseph G. Turner, Michael McCosh. I was only 3 years old at the time. I have never known any of her friends from that time, what happened that day and what she was like as a person. If you can help me learn anything about her or that day please contact me at Miki@.....*

The post alone is enough to bring tears to your eyes. Miki was looking for any information about the mother she didn't remember. Charmian Cliff is my wife's maiden name and not only was she jumping with Carolyn Reynolds that afternoon but she also worked for her. Charmian had temporarily accepted the job of nanny for Carolyn's three daughters and her husband's two children while they made arrangements for a permanent caretaker. I remember the afternoon very well. I was flying the Cessna 180 and though I had been flying parachute jumpers over four years, this was the first time I had flown someone who lost a life.

I gave the information to Charmian and she immediately picked up her cell phone and dialed the number. Miki answered the phone and they talked for over an hour. Miki, her husband, Willie, and her five-year-old son, Cooper, live in Salida, Colorado, just west of Pueblo and Charmian and I vowed that we would fly up to Salida to see her the next time we flew the Cessna 195 to Colorado. We found out that after Carolyn died, Miki and her two sisters had been raised by her grandfather and grandmother in Aurora, Colorado. Once they were 18 years old, grandfather told them they would have to fend for themselves from then on. He still lovingly guided them along their way but essentially they were on their own. Miki managed to find a job and worked her way through college, received her degree, and now had a good job in Denver that allowed her to live in Salida.

That phone call took place in March 2010 and we were in the middle of negotiating the sale of our hangar/residence in Texas and trying to relocate to a suitable place in Denver. We didn't find the opportunity to meet Miki until we completed our relocation. In August, right after Oshkosh, we called Miki but she was not going to be home the next weekend. Undeterred, Charmian kept trying to find a free moment when we could meet Miki and her family and tell her what we could of her mother, Carolyn.

Finally, Friday afternoon, 13th of August, 2010 everything seemed to come together and we pulled the 195 out of the hangar for a nine a.m. departure. Miki wasn't going to get off work until two p.m. and it was only a 55-minute flight over the mountains southwest of Denver, but I try to leave fairly early when heading west out of Denver. There was 55 gallons of fuel in the tanks so I wasn't worried about performance and I estimated it would be enough to fly the round trip and take the family for a short sightseeing ride if they elected to do so.

The flight was nothing short of glorious. Colorado in August is usually beautiful and this Friday lived up to its reputation. The air was smooth, the mountains magnificent. The Salida airport was virtually deserted when we arrived but finally another pilot walked around the hangar and was drawn to our highly polished 195 like a magnet. We asked about transportation into town and he directed us to the empty FBO where a sign-in sheet needed to be filled out and we were welcome to any of the three courtesy cars in the parking lot.

We picked the best looking car and hopped in. Guess what? It ran fine but the obligatory yellow "Check Engine" light glowed steadily in the panel. Have you ever driven an airport courtesy car without the "check engine" light being on? I haven't.

Salida isn't a large town but we found a nice place for lunch then drove into the old town and parked along the Arkansas River. We walked around for an hour or so until Miki called and said she would meet us in the park.

I started to notice a few butterflies flying around in my stomach about then, maybe this wasn't going to be as easy as I thought. In about 15 minutes Miki and Willie walked up and welcomed us to Salida. We found a nice bar across the street and while Willie and Miki drank a beer I nursed a diet coke in case I got to go flying again and we proceeded to try to get to know each other a little.

It turned out to be a delightful afternoon. Charmian and Miki were instantly bonded together in conversation about Miki's mother. Willie and I talked about his welding business and his passion with rafting along the Arkansas River. We finished up at the bar and drove to their house to meet five-year-old son Cooper who was just out of school for the day. He was a delightful young man who seemed well suited in the family that absolutely adored him.

Rafting on the Arkansas River on a warm August Colorado afternoon.

Miki and Willie showed us their river raft and suggested we drag it down to the river and go for a ride. It took an hour to position the cars and get the raft into the river. We enjoyed the warm summer afternoon on the Arkansas River.

It was about two hours until sundown when we finished storing the raft back at the house and Miki expressed an interest in flying in the plane. We all loaded back into our cars and headed for the airport. The winds were still up a little, but not enough to be really rough around the mountains so I pre-flighted the 195 and began the briefing with my three passengers,

Charmian would stay on the airport so the backseat would be more comfortable for Willie and Cooper.

The Hodge family taking in the experience of small airplane flying in our Cessna 195. Miki, Willie, and Cooper.

Cooper was getting a little antsy in the rear seat so I invited him to come up front where he could see better.

We flew down the Arkansas River, retracing our raft trip earlier in the afternoon, then back over Salida and marveled at the mountains surrounding the countryside. Cooper was a little antsy in the backseat. He had long ago unbuckled his seatbelt and he was alternating between the left and right windows trying to take in the sights. I invited him to walk up between the seats and sit on Miki's lap so he could see ahead a little better. As soon as he sat down his little hands reached for the control wheel but Miki quickly snatched them up and off and looked at me apologetically.

Little Cooper at the controls of the Cessna 195 over Salida, Colorado.

I just laughed and told her it would be alright for him to handle the controls. I don't think she believed me, but she did turn loose of his hands and he grabbed the control wheel again. Cooper moved the wheel gently left to see what would happen while I pressed the left rudder to help bank the airplane. When he realized he was controlling the airplane his eyes lit up and a big smile spread across his face. He wasted no time increasing the bank then leveling out while contemplating what he had just done and what to do next. It didn't take long for him to figure that out. He very firmly rolled the airplane back and forth and I followed up with the rudder and watched him break out into another delighted smile. I let him roll back and forth for a few minutes then sort of nudged the nose down to gain some speed and pitched up into a gentle wingover to the left. He wasn't so sure about the wingover at first and glanced back and forth but almost immediately started laughing and giggling with delight as the ground came back into view on the left side.

I think he would have continued banking back and forth for an hour if we would have let him but I began to notice signs of distress from Miki and I thought she probably had experienced enough of flying for this evening. We asked Cooper to go back to his seat and put on his seatbelt for the landing. After securing the airplane for the night we headed to the hotel to get cleaned up for dinner.

We met back at Miki's house and as I walked past little Cooper's room I noticed he was finishing up his macaroni and cheese. When he saw me he immediately jumped up and ran to me. He grabbed my left hand and each of his little hands wrapped tightly around two of my fingers and dragged me to the far wall of his room. He then released one hand, still holding me with the other, and with a loud crash, pulled a box full of toys off of the shelf. The toys scattered across the floor and when I looked down I realized this was his box of airplanes. He then pulled me down so I would sit with him and patiently picked up each airplane, one at a time, and showed each one to me, each time he would smile and exclaim, "See this one?" I would acknowledge each airplane and tell him what kind of airplane it was. I could see he already knew what they were and he would agree with me with a broad smile. Now I knew there was a cold beer waiting for me in the kitchen but that could wait, I didn't want to miss a single minute with this delightful child and he continued showing me his treasures until they all were identified and returned to their box.

Soon enough I got to my beer and after finishing it we left the house and walked to the restaurant in town and sat down for a memorable dinner with Miki and her family. I wish I could have been privy to the quiet conversation between Charmian and Miki that afternoon and during dinner, but Miki did eventually turn to me and asked me what I knew about her mother. I told her that I had just gotten out of the Air Force a couple of months before the accident and didn't know her mother very well. She then asked what her mood was before getting on the airplane for that fateful jump. I told her I did recall she was smiling broadly when she boarded the airplane, like most skydivers, and was kidding and laughing with Charmian and the other two skydivers jumping with her.

Miki seemed relieved for a moment, and then she asked me, "So, do you think she committed suicide on that jump?"

This took me back a little at first, I told her in no uncertain terms that her mother absolutely did not commit suicide that day. She had died accidentally. The look of relief in Miki's eyes told volumes as she related that her grandfather, who had raised her and her two sisters after Carolyn died, had often said that he wondered if his daughter caused her own death that day. I reiterated that was not the case. For some unknown reason her mother was unable to deploy either of her two parachutes.

Suicides are virtually unheard of in skydiving, most skydivers were so full of life they rarely thought of it and would do anything to avoid it. Most would say: "I'm not really afraid to die, but I am afraid of not living." Living life to the fullest is what most skydivers are doing, generally speaking they do not have a death wish and even though they do take chances, they invariably are constantly evaluating the odds of having an accident against the thrill of putting their selves at risk and doing everything possible to keep those odds in their favor. I think Miki was able to put to rest one of the nagging questions she had been contemplating most of her life.

The next day our flight back to Denver was as enjoyable as the day before and as we pushed the old airplane back into the hangar we contemplated what we had just done. Sure, the flight in our Cessna 195 was, as usual, very enjoyable, but the thought of being able to meet with Miki and maybe help her to understand a little more about her mother eclipsed the flying. If we could help her come to terms with losing Carolyn so early in her life then we may have accomplished something of value, it certainly made the flight more important to us.

For me, the highlight was seeing little Cooper's broad smile as we rolled back and forth in the 195 over Salida. Then, when he grabbed my hand and dragged me into his bedroom, despite my determination to continue into the kitchen for my beer is a memory I will cherish forever.

Flying back to Denver after our wonderful experience meeting Miki and her family.

We vowed to keep in touch with Miki and her family and hope to have them over soon. I can't wait to take little Cooper up in the J-3. The Cessna 195 made this trip a lot more memorable. It has never been said better than by Kent Blankenberg:

"In the sky our hearts beat faster when we admire the enduring loveliness of a particular airplane which for one reason or another achieves the status of a standard of perfection. It is the quality of enduring value that defines something as a classic, rather than being a passing fancy. The Cessna 195, Cessna's "Business Liner" possesses these qualities."

Charmian and I videoed our flight in Salida while Cooper was flying the Cessna 195. This touching video can be viewed at the following link:

https://www.youtube.com/watch?v=8n1oWMchWfc

It is also possible to see the video if you go to YouTube and ask for: Cessna 195 flown by Cooper.

17

ONCE I FLEW A DC-8
(For about 7 Years)

There was no moon tonight but the stars burned so brilliantly in the northern sky they illuminated the cockpit. Our lights were turned down and we could see the Big Dipper slowly rotating around the North Star, the first officer was gazing out of the windshield and I was leaning back in my seat listening to classical music from some station tuned on the ADF. I didn't know who the composer of this piece was but I knew it was a Russian artist, we were 75 miles east of Kamchatka Peninsula and only Russian music would be broadcast in this area. The four Pratt and Whitney fan jets were churning the cold outside air relentlessly leaving a long white trail of vapor that must have shown dimly in the starlight, it was unlikely anyone was around the North Pacific Ocean to observe it though.

We had left Yakota Air Force Base, Japan a few hours after sunset and were bound for McChord AFB outside of Tacoma, Washington in the US. There were no passengers on board this stretched DC 8-63 and we had very little idea what had been loaded on the pallets strapped securely behind us. The military paid for this charter flight each week and there were rumors about what we carried, but never any real confirmation of what it was. There was the tale of a roll of heavy chain shipped back and forth so the commanders could point out how much they needed this charter, but I had never seen the roll of chain on my aircraft. Most likely we carried personal effects for the military families relocating to or from Japan or some supplies for the troops that were sorely needed for one reason or another. Still, it was fun to speculate.

The autopilot kept us on altitude and heading. Occasionally we would change the heading bug left or right to keep us within the boundaries of our assigned track. Every couple of hours we would call Tokyo Control on the HF radio and give them our position report as we crossed the reporting points. Each time we would check our fuel burn, ETA, and confirm there would be about 15000 pounds of jet fuel remaining in the tanks on our arrival. At each reporting fix you could see the Big Dipper had rotated further around the North Star. All of the other constellations I was able to identify were following dutifully in their elegant dance around the Northern Hemisphere's only stationary star.

Even though the nose of the DC-8 held steady on the heading we established upon entering our assigned track, by midnight the compass heading had already started to swing to the east. It was the way it worked on the routes called the great circle. You started out heading almost straight north, at the halfway point the compass heading had changed to east, and shortly before arrival it showed a south heading but the actual initial heading established on the track never changed more than a few degrees. The flight engineer and I dutifully logged the differences along our route and compared everything to our flight plan. We were especially diligent during the first five hours of this flight. Only a month before the Soviets had murdered 269 innocent people by shooting down Korean Air 007, a 747 that had inadvertently strayed over Sakhalin Island. That's why I had tuned the ADF to the classical music; it gave us some assurance of our relative position to the unknown station. Our weather radar was pointed downward and we were watching the Kurile Islands on the scope using the terrain feature, keeping them far to the left of us until passing well north when we would start painting the Aleutian Island chain.

Before leaving the hotel all three of us debriefed the incoming crew. By the time we headed to the airport they were well into their second Kirin beers and settling in for the one week layover until the next charter flight arrived. We had enjoyed our week in Japan, probably drank too much Kirin at the hotel. No doubt we drank too much the evening we spent in Tokyo, sampling sake and beer. Ah, the Japanese people were so respectful and polite, somehow we woke up the next afternoon in our hotel rooms.

The takeoff from Yakota had been tense but fairly routine. We arrived at operations an hour before departure to prepare for the flight. As usual, we would be at maximum gross weight at the start of takeoff. The Yakota runway was over two miles long and we would utilize virtually all of it before lifting off. There was no chance to reduce our takeoff weight by reducing our fuel load because we were heading to the foggy northwest US in February. Fog was indeed forecast for our arrival at sunrise. The flight engineer, Jon, left the operations office to walk around the DC-8 and supervise the fueling.

Another load of cargo passing through the wide cargo door on the Douglas DC-8.

Jim, the first officer, was computing our weight and balance paperwork. Tonight it was easy because we would be full. The Air Force loadmasters were good about distributing the weight evenly and they knew just how much they could upload on the DC-8. When we saw the final manifest I was a little disappointed to confirm there would be no room for additional fuel, but the flight plan estimated our arrival fuel at 15,000 pounds. That would allow for about 20 minutes of holding before we would have to divert from McChord to SeaTac airport in case of fog. Usually you could count on at least one of them staying above landing minimums at sunrise and there were several alternates we could use to the north around Vancouver. Any diversion for weather was an expensive event for the company, the Department of Defense didn't pay extra for diversions so the company had to add that cost when you bid for the route contract. If you included too much, someone else got the route and your airplanes may be sitting for the duration, which was even more expensive. That was above my expertise. All I needed to worry about is getting to McChord in one piece along with the DC-8 and the rest of the crew and cargo.

Author, Mike Larson, "dripping the fuel tanks" on the DC-8 when he served as a flight engineer.

About 15 minutes before start time Jim and I walked out to the airplane, we noticed Jon dripping the last of the six fuel tanks to check mechanically how much fuel was actually on board. He was furloughed from Flying Tigers Airline and Jon was one of the most professional engineers I had ever flown with. He had checked the fuel on board before beginning loading additional fuel, computed how much it would take to bring it up to our flight planned load and then monitored the upload on the gauges on the Flight Engineer's panel located behind the First Officer's seat.

When the fueler brought the fuel slip to the cockpit, Jon recomputed the fueler's report, checked it with his computations and against the gages and if everything balanced against each of the figures he would head under the wing to do the mechanical check as well. When Jon told you there was 136,500 pounds (a little over 20,000 gallons) of fuel on board you could trust that number because you knew Jon was one of the good ones. The mechanical check was called "dripping the tanks." It was a pain in the butt and messy, invariably fuel spilled onto your hands and sometimes uniform and it would stink of jet fuel in the cockpit all the way to the U.S.

When a flight engineer re-entered the cockpit for the final time and stank of fuel, you knew he was doing his job. You would get used to the smell and not notice it shortly after takeoff. Not all of our flight engineers were that conscientious about this job, it didn't pay half of what they earned at their previous airlines and the job was much more demanding at a non-scheduled charter airline. You would adjust your relationship with each flight engineer depending on how much you trusted him. Jon walked in stinking to high heaven, handed me his paperwork and the fuel slip so I could check them against the totals I had come up with in operations. You could also rely on Jon to hide a few thousand extra pounds of fuel somewhere in all of those tanks. Some day we would need it.

I took my seat and began to make my nest for the ten-and-a-half hour journey across the North Pacific Ocean. With everything set up, the First Officer and I rechecked the route in the INSs (inertial reference systems) against the flight plan paperwork. Each fix had to be entered by their east and north coordinates, each coordinate started with either an East or North (until crossing the date line, then a West coordinate was used) and then a six-digit number with decimal points, there were approximately twenty-five coordinates along our route and each one was checked over and over again until we were sure they were correct. Even though the investigation had not been completed on the Korean Air 747 that was shot down last month, anyone who flew this route knew the crew had probably just entered one or two wrong numbers out of the hundreds and the autopilot flew the airplane over Russia instead of down along the Pacific tracks. That isn't going to happen tonight.

With the route check done and verified and the checklists complete I call the ground crew and ask for start clearance on engine three. They open the valve on the air cart that sends 30 psi air pressure through the plumbing in the DC-8. I pushed the number three over head start button and all three of us listen to the start sequence. I wish I could add the sound effects of the engine start on a DC-8 to this story. The whistling and whining heard up in the cockpit is unique in aviation and anyone having heard it will never forget it.

When the pneumatic starter opens on the fan jet, initially there is a rush of air escaping from the engine and the air cart powers up to keep the pressure above the minimum. It takes a few seconds to spool the engine up to about 15%, and then we push the fuel lever forward. The rush of air outside is gradually replaced by an increasing whine as the engine spools up. When the fuel ignites, a dull roar begins and the whine of the engine gets louder. It is an overpowering roar out on the ramp but up here in the cockpit it is just loud enough to reassure us that everything is progressing nicely. When engine speed reached 60 percent the starter button automatically pops out and disengages the start valve, the air duct pressure rises and confirms the start valve closure. The air cart is still screaming outside and as soon as number three stabilizes and we get clearance from the ground crew to start number two and repeat as above.

You started these two engines first because they have the hydraulic pumps then proceed to four then one. Jon is busy during the start bringing the generators on line, checking fuel pressures, hydraulics, fire warning systems, and oil pressures. With all four engines up and stabilized we cleared the ground crew to disconnect, pull the chocks and get out of the way. When the after start check list is complete the First Officer calls Yakota ground for taxi clearance. I glance at the airport diagram to confirm where they want us to taxi, look out the window for one more check of the weather (the visibility is still hanging around a mile), return the salute to the ground crew and thank my lucky stars I'm up here and not down in the humid 34° weather.

It takes a lot of power to start the 355,000 pounds of DC-8 rolling across the damp ramp, the First Officer yelled "Clear right!" over the roar and I turned the nose-steering wheel gently to the right and headed for the end of the active runway. When we were positively on the right taxiway we accomplished the taxi check and then held short of the active, awaiting our takeoff clearance.

"Big A 3746 you are cleared to takeoff runway 29, turn right to heading 310, climb and maintain 8,000 feet." I increased the power and turned the grossed out Douglas onto the runway while the First Officer repeated our clearance and Jon was going through our final takeoff checklist.

Jon announced, "Takeoff check is complete and we're cleared for takeoff!"

It was the First Officer's turn to fly this leg so as soon as the airplane is stopped and lined up on the runway I turned the controls over to him. He acknowledged he has the airplane and started to slowly move the throttles forward while still holding the brakes. Jon has moved his seat up between us where he can better monitor the front engine instruments and when all four engines are spooled and stable he announced to that effect. The First Officer released the brakes and brings the engines up to full power then raised his hands just above the throttles while Jon made the final adjustments and when he says, "power set" the First Officer grasps the throttles again, always ready to shut them down if one of us sees something wrong and orders to abort the takeoff.

Now this is the most critical part of the next ten and a half hours. This has to be done right and we are all intensely monitoring the airplane, each other, the miles of runway ahead that is visible, and listening to every sound, every nuance that the old DC-8 has taught us over the years. In the early part of the takeoff it would be easy to abort and roll to a stop on the long runway, but every second we delay, the complexity and ramifications of an aborted takeoff multiply exponentially against a successful outcome.

At first the acceleration is slow and lumbering, it's almost like the tires are out of round as we accelerated unevenly until reaching about 50 knots. My first callout is at 80 knots and the First Officer gently pushed the stick forward a couple of inches and we all checked to see the nose lower slightly then recover to level. This assured us the control tab on the elevator is free and working properly, and we continued. The runway lights were starting to pass by more quickly and at about 100 knots the end of the runway is in sight. Damn, that's half the runway gone already and we have to gain a lot more speed before we can lift off.

Fortunately, this is where the fan jets really are more efficient and the acceleration increased significantly. My next call out is V-1 (take-off decision speed). At that moment the First Officer will remove his hand from the throttles and we are committed to flying the airplane whether something fails or not, there was no longer enough room to stop. Frankly, every time I do this, when we reach V-1, I've had serious doubts about our ability to stop way before then. If something happened, I would dutifully abort the takeoff before V-1 and hope for the best and so far everything the book said this airplane can do has been accurate.

Douglas DC-8 taxiing to the runway.

I'll tell you though, it would be tough to stop this much weight in what little runway is left just before V-1. About 15 knots later we accelerated to V-R (rotation speed), it was time to transition into the air but this airplane doesn't just jump into the air. The First Officer gently raises the nose to 8° pitch and holds it there. His eyes are no longer looking outside. On this runway at 8° pitch, the end of the runway disappears under the nose and you are on instruments while still rolling along the ground. It's kind of unnerving for the brief time you are in this predicament and everyone has a tendency to increase the pitch to lift off but you can't do that in a stretched DC-8 or you'll jam the tail skid onto the runway and that raises all kind of havoc. I know, I've done it.

When I was a co-pilot we took off from Yakota one evening and after I felt the wheels lift off I rotated a little more and the tail skid hit, the whole airplane shook and rumbled loudly. Captain Strong just about jumped out of his seat (as did I) and grabbed the top of the instrument panel with both hands. Then he turned to me and said, "I think you hit the tail skid, Mikey!"

I said I was sorry, but I thought once we were in the air I could rotate to climb pitch. He said that usually you could but not if you rotated that aggressively. I never did again. To add insult, the tower called and told us they thought they observed us hit the tail. Maybe it was the copious shower of sparks following us as we lifted off that got their attention.

Clyde Strong and the old crusty flight engineer had both cut their teeth at Airlift International and been around the world many times. These guys had some sand and they were not about to let this situation go to waste. I had only been with the charter airline a couple of months and I wasn't sure what company policy was when this happened, I guess it depended on how much damage had occurred. There were measurements on the tail strut and if it had compressed beyond a certain point it would have to be replaced. For the next ten and a half hours all I heard was it was the hardest tail strike they had ever experienced and that it had been, "Nice knowing you, Mikey!"

I thought I was going to get fired. Man I sweated that flight out until we landed at McChord and I could see what damage I had done. When we finished the parking check list I headed for the door but Clyde was blocking it while he slowly put on his uniform coat, he was savoring the moment. The engineer was steadily writing in the log book what I thought was my death sentence at this airline. I HAD to check that tail skid. I followed Clyde as he slowly strolled down the stairs at half speed, he was relishing every second of my torment.

The mechanic greeted us about half way down the air stair. Smiling, he said, "Well, hello Clyde, how was the flight?"

"Hey, Bill, it was pretty smooth, by the way, we must have scraped some paint off the tail skid, do you have a can of spray paint handy?"

"Sure thing Clyde, it's in the truck, I'll take care of it." And that was the last I ever heard of it! When I checked the skid I couldn't believe the violence we felt and the sparks reported by the tower resulted in just a little missing paint.

The very next week we were taking off from Yakota on the same charter. This time I was with a different crew and the captain was making the takeoff. As soon as we lifted off I could feel him rotate a little too aggressively and exactly the same thing happened, the loud whump and the eventual call from the tower. I didn't try to make the captain squirm like I had been forced to do. I confessed what happened to me last week. The flight engineer made a feeble attempt at lecturing him but he was a young inexperienced refugee from Tigers and the captain was having none of it. Interestingly, in seven years operating DC-8s those are the only two tail strikes I saw, both only a week apart

---

Shortly after rotating and losing sight of the runway ahead, it seemed like an eternity before liftoff. I'm sure it was only a second or two but you could feel the tires still rotating on the pavement, then the oleo struts would extend, and finally the old girl would lift off. We would let her accelerate just a little, slowly pulling the nose up when we were sure the skid would clear the ground and then, at the first indication on the vertical speed indicator call, "Positive rate, gear up." I reached over the console and placed the long gear handle in the up position and listened to the nose gear stow in the cavity. As soon as the gear doors closed all of the gear lights turned off and we were on our way. At a thousand feet we would raise the flaps half way and accelerate to about 230 knots and finally retract the flap to full up.

A DC-8 felt like a ton of rocks slowly climbing and gaining speed while turning to our initial heading. We check in with Tokyo on the radio and they cleared us to our cruise altitude without delay. After intercepting a VOR radial that will take us clear of the commercial traffic we are cleared direct to our initial entry point for our assigned track. Not all takeoffs were as smooth.

One night we were departing on this flight and the tower called to report they observed quite a few sparks coming from our number two engine. While I scanned the engine instruments on number two, seeing if I could find anything unusual, I told them that it was probably normal to see a few sparks from the engines on takeoff. Everything seemed okay until the engineer pointed to the throttle. It was a full knob width forward of the other three throttle levers and then told me, "You know, I had to keep pushing that one up to maintain takeoff power!" I still wasn't too concerned but thought this is worth checking out further. Right then an Air Force C-130 called and volunteered to fly along side of us to take a look at the left side of the airplane.

We agreed, thinking he would intercept, see nothing and we would be on our way. In fact, when alongside he reported all looked normal. I was greatly relieved to hear that, all engine instruments were still in the green and the throttle position of number two a little forward was the only indication of anything abnormal. I decided, however, to check number two at takeoff power and radioed the C-130 to keep an eye out while I advanced the throttle. I pulled the other engines back slightly then carefully moved two up. Just as it reach full power the engine started vibrating so much the instruments became a blur and the engine started losing power. At the same time the C-130 driver radioed, "You've got 50 feet of flames from number two and that doesn't appear normal to me!" By the time he finished his statement I had pulled the throttle to idle and we began shutting it down. As soon as the power came back the vibration stopped and the C-130 said the flames had stopped, he would standby for further assistance. We notified Tokyo Control of our intention to return to Yakota but we would have to dump fuel to reduce landing weight. The first officer continued flying the airplane and even on three engines he managed to keep a shallow climb while I and the flight engineer completed all of the checklists. I switched radio frequencies for radar vectors to the dump area over Mount Fuji. It took about a half hour to unload all of that fuel, we received vectors back to Yakota and, as required, I took control of the DC-8 and landed.

I had always thought this event was a great triumph in my flying career. We had taken off in a fully loaded DC-8 from a foreign airport and experienced an engine failure. The crew and I had successfully managed the emergency, dumped thousands of gallons of fuel over Mt. Fuji, and returned the old airplane back to the airport. We returned to the hotel with a tantalizing story to tell over a cold Kirin.

Well, all of that did happen, but as I write this I realize how mundane it really was. All of us on the crew had been through this several times in DC-8 simulators at the United Airlines training center and there was very little difference in the actual event. There was always the knowledge that, unlike in the simulator, our well being was really on the line this time if we screwed it up, but we just followed the same procedures as if it was another training event and all ended well. It was embarrassing whenever someone complimented me about our job since it was really no big deal.

This was the last of four engine failures or precautionary shutdown in seven years flying "8s" and none of them were any sweat. All three happened right at or just after takeoff and except for the last one they were just barely noticeable by any of us on the crew. The first was just after liftoff from Denver on the way to Kansas City. The captain felt a little yaw and just said, "What happened to number three?"

We cleaned up the airplane, completed the checklist and carried on to Kansas City. There, the mechanics determined the accessory drive had failed which cut off fuel pressure to the engine, thus the flame out. This was the one and only time I exercised my mechanics license (A&P) on the DC-8. I determined the airplane was safe for a three-engine ferry, signed my name and A/P number in the logbook, and watched the mechanics stuff two by fours in between the guide vanes and engine blades of engine three. This was to prevent the engine from turning while we flew the airplane. They secured them with rope, and assured me they do this all of the time. I remember two other precautionary engine shut downs and they were mainly non-events as well.

We took off on three engines and an hour and a half later landed at company headquarters at Willow Run Airport, Ypsilanti, Michigan. I was really excited about this flight, talk about the big time, I had arrived. Only a year earlier I was spraying cotton with a Piper Pawnee in Arizona. I used to glance at the airliners approaching Sky Harbor Airport outside of

Phoenix thinking that was a neat job but they couldn't possibly be having as much fun as I was. Then I would duck under the power lines at the end of the field and wrench the Pawnee around and fall back into the cotton. I did this for three years and it is literally the hardest job I've ever done. It wasn't the flying, it was the hours of preparation and clean up and maintenance, it was the effect of the chemicals after months of exposure every summer, but most of all it was the fatigue from sleeping only a few hours each night, returning to the airport before sunrise with only a nap in the afternoon, and back into the Pawnee until just after sundown.

Author serving as a DC-8 flight engineer.

That's why I was so excited about my new job as a flight engineer on a DC-8. I first went to work for Rosenbalm Aviation in Ypsilanti. We were on call 24 hours a day, seven days a week,. If you drank a beer, you were taking a chance of missing a flight. Once you were called, if you turned the flight down you were placed on the bottom of the list and it may be a couple days before you would get another call. Since I was new to the airplane I wanted to fly as much as I could. I was a good pilot but this was a different kind of aviation than I was used to. The company had hired me over the phone on the recommendation of my friend Randy. He had assured them that I was a good pilot. After all, I had checked Randy out in the Beech 18 when he was a kid in college. Randy was well regarded at the company and I had taught him!

Well they were so impressed that they let me bypass the engineer seat and moved me into the right seat. Unfortunately, I had only just gotten my instrument ticket a few months earlier and had no idea how to fly instruments in a DC-8 or anything else but a Cessna 172. After a few disastrous attempts at non-precision approaches in the simulator they figured that out. I was very graciously offered a try in the engineer's seat. My engineer's ticket was brand new as well but even though the engineer's job is as important as the pilots', it wasn't as demanding and I passed the minimum standards so they kept me on.

The second engine failure was an accessory drive problem as well. It was on climb out from LAX. There was very little indication the engine failed, the nose dropped a little and the rate of climb decreased slightly. We were about 12,000 feet when we noticed the number three engine instruments rolling back to idle, then zero. We pressed on to Dayton, Ohio at a slightly lower altitude than we flight planned and landed with about the original flight planned fuel. The third engine shutdown was caused by a fire warning while climbing through 3,000 feet after departing Port-au-Prince, Haiti. We dutifully shut it down and completed the Engine/Fire Shutdown Checklist and proceeded on to Miami. We were pretty certain it was a fire warning system failure and that was confirmed in Miami.

After departure from Yakota we would receive clearance from Tokyo Control telling us which route we would take, then check everything on the flight plan one more time and head for the entry point. The old DC-8 would lumber along, slowly climbing. Some pilots would hand-fly the airplane until around 18,000 ft., then turn on the autopilot for the rest of the flight until landing. You had to watch the airspeed carefully because if you let it slow more than a few knots below climb speed you would have to level off, sometimes for five or ten minutes before it would accelerate back to speed. You would lose valuable time climbing to altitude, causing an increase in fuel consumption. Not a good way to start the flight. If you held the airspeed, the old girl would slowly but steadily climb to your initial cruise altitude which was often initially below 30,000 ft. because of the heavy weight. You didn't want a DC-8 too high when she was this heavy. If you got slow because of mismanagement or turbulence she not only wouldn't climb but she would try to come back down to an altitude that was more comfortable, whether you wanted to or not! After a few hours, as the fuel was consumed and the weight was reduced, you could start climbing to a higher, more fuel efficient altitude

ID card required to be displayed during the Emery Air Freight contract.

One of my first flights as an engineer was an overnight to JFK, the weather was crappy and we had to shoot an approach just before sunrise down to minimums in icing and turbulence. I let out such a sigh of relief when we saw the end of the runway and touched down, both the Captain and First Officer laughed at me. I'd heard of this kind of flying but this was the first I'd ever witnessed and it impressed me. When we taxied back to the ramp and shut down I walked around the airplane for my post flight inspection. I could hear a strange sounding airplane approaching the runway and looked up just in time to watch the British Airways Concord break out of the overcast and touchdown right in front of me. WOW, am I an airline geek now or what!

I spent two long years as a flight engineer with a couple of months on furlough. During the furlough I was lucky to get on with Connie Kalletta flying his turbine Beech 18s and that was where I finally figured out how to fly instruments. Connie would walk into the office and see you on the phone checking weather and he would chew you out, "You're going anyway, why do you care about the weather!" Kalletta was kind of angry when I notified him I was recalled back to Rosenbalm and I would not be able to fly for him any longer.

Those two years were invaluable when it came time for another try in the right seat and I finally figured out how to pass the check ride. By the time I flew another year as a first officer, I was officially a DC-8 pilot. Of course, the first thing I did then was, quit.

A charter company (Arrow Air) was hiring current and qualified DC-8 crew to fly passenger charters from the west coast to Europe. No more flying boxes for me and I was going to learn to fly overseas! I gave Rosenbalm's chief pilot a one - week notice and he was mad as heck. He lamented, "You know how tight we run our crews, I need at least a month notice!" I told him, "No can do, ground school starts in nine days!" He got even angrier and said, "Alright, you're off the next trip, turn in your stuff and I'm going to put in your record you quit without notice." I guess he didn't remember when I answered the phone (on three different occasions) expecting a trip assignment but the secretary merely said I was furloughed as of this moment until further notice. Three times in two years!

I managed to get through the Arrow ground school in Denver and easily passed the First Officer check ride (it was a piece of cake, they needed pilots) and received my first assignment.

Six month old daughter, Laura, coming on board to say goodbye before we departed.

I reported to SFO for a late evening departure to London Gatwick. I bummed a ride from LAX to SFO on Air Cal the night before and checked out the local area for the first time. The next afternoon it took me 45 minutes to find where the DC-8 was supposed to depart and finally located the Arrow Air operations, beating my check Captain by only a few minutes, good thing I checked out of the hotel early. Captain McInerny was a heavy smoker and a refugee from the now-defunct Airlift International. He had indeed been around the world a few times.

I had never flown more than a four-hour leg, left the US, or been concerned about flight attendants or passengers for that matter. He carefully walked me through the preflight, filing an international flight plan, working out the weight and balance, and showing me the route we would be flying over the North Atlantic in about six hours after takeoff from SFO. I was jazzed, excited, and scared at the same time. Captain McInerny was cool and calm and just smiled and shook his head at me while he lit up yet another cigarette.

I knew I was fortunate the weather was going to be decent when we landed at Gatwick so I tried to gather up some courage and calm down and be a little more like the Captain while we walked down the concourse to the DC-8. It was loud in the gateway, I couldn't even hear anything being said, that is when I realized it was raining so hard outside the visibility was down to a quarter mile. I really hadn't paid attention to the weather in SFO while doing the paperwork. So much for my cool and confident composure. The flight attendant could sense it the second I said hello. She looked at the Captain and F/E and kidded them about the new guy. I managed to get all of my stuff in reasonable order and we started engines and began the long taxi in the quarter mile visibility. I was lost immediately but Captain McInerny just kept the airplane moving and lighting one cigarette after another. He finally stopped and locked the brakes at the end of some runway and began discussing the interest rate on the CD he just bought with his retirement from Airlift with the engineer.

I looked off to my right into the dark evening twilight at what looked like about a quarter mile of runway in the heavy rain and I was sweating bullets about getting this thing off the ground in this weather.

Emery Air Freight contract DC-8.

"BIG A 2978 you are cleared for takeoff runway 09L"

I just about jumped out of my skin. Did they actually think we were going to take off in this crap? Captain McInerny stuffed the cigarette into his mouth and brought up the power to taxi onto the runway. He glared at me until I keyed the mike and acknowledged our takeoff clearance.

Okay, so this crazy pilot thinks we're really going to get airborne in this stuff, I'm sure he's done it before so I relax a little and decide to try to learn something watching him perform this miracle. That's when he let go of the throttles and the idiot said, "Okay Mike, it's your airplane, let's go!" Wait....WHAT?

I'm no longer thinking straight, I don't feel good about this, and I don't really want to go to England anymore. So, I grab a hand full of throttles and carefully push them up to takeoff power. My eyes are glued to the center line as they gradually start passing underneath the nose of the DC-8 until they become a blur. I've checked the elevator at 80 knots and impatiently wait for the airspeed to build up. I haven't the slightest idea how far the end of the runway is but we are going so fast now that the quarter mile visibility seems like only a few feet. Finally, we reach V-1, then V-R and I gently raise the nose to 8° degrees pitch and hold it there. The runway is no longer visible and I am steering by the compass when I feel the oleo struts begin to extend and then a faint "clunk" as they extend fully and we are, thankfully, off the runway. I hold this attitude faithfully until the Captain says, "Positive Rate of Climb."

Somehow I managed to squeak, "Gear Up," wishing I had something to relieve the dryness in my mouth. I can now raise the nose up to maintain climb speed and call for the flaps and after takeoff check as if I know what I'm doing. The engineer was saying something, and laughing about his CDs that were maturing in a matter of a couple of months, his hands were flying about his panel and the throttles, he wasn't even nervous. Up around 10,000 feet I began to realize we actually made it. I relaxed my grip on the control wheel and tried to get my shoulders to relax a little bit. The Captain and flight engineer were still engaged in their financial strategies as I started to realize what just happened. We were on our way to Jolly Old England. We broke out of the clouds around 18,000 feet and they began to break up below us. The Sierra Nevada Mountains were gleaming in the moonshine and once again I remembered, this is just another airplane flight, maybe a little different from anything I've done before, but after that takeoff, how much harder can it be?

I'll never forget the first time listening to Speed Bird (British Airways) following us across the northern US, calling Canadian Control for our clearance above Sault Ste. Marie, the Northern Lights illuminating the cockpit for the first time, and receiving our clearance onto the North Atlantic Track from Gander Control. That first Atlantic sunrise at 20 West is seared into my brain and the first English accented radio clearance is never to be forgotten. While descending into the majestic English countryside on that bright morning became almost commonplace to me over the years, the first time it was as exciting and magical as anything I've ever experienced. The approach and landing at Gatwick was completed without any of the anxieties experienced on the takeoff the night before and even the trip to the hotel was memorable.

As we climbed north away from Tokyo we were really on edge. There was a half hour or so when the only navigation tool we had was the Omega low-frequency receiver. It was pretty accurate over water and at night but you never wanted to have only one source to keep you on course. As Tokyo receded behind us and the last ADF signal faded, our only other backup was finding some ADF transmitter out of Russia and make sure it stayed to your left and kept swinging properly. Eventually the Kurile Islands would appear on the upper left of the radar screen and you could relax somewhat as that was confirming your position. Jon would keep a steady stream of barely warm coffee, poured from the thermos, handed up to us as we counted down the hours.

Working for Arrow Air was an incredible experience, when you listened to the ex-airline pilots complain about how bad it was at the non-scheds and how good it is at the big guys you would think it was a crummy job but it wasn't. I know now those same pilots complained just as much no matter where they worked. At Arrow, when you reported for a flight, they gave you a DC-8 full of jet fuel and told you what your heading should be after takeoff and, when there was only about 15,000 lb. of fuel left after anywhere from six to 12 hours, where to land. Usually we went to a nice hotel and waited for them to tell us where to go next. If something changed along the way it was up to you to get yourself and the crew to a safe place. If there were maintenance issues, you made the arrangements to get it resolved.

Arrow had a contract with KLM to fly passengers from Paramaribo, Surinam on the east coast of South America to Amsterdam. The flight would refuel and change crew in San Juan. I was assigned to fly the southbound leg from San Juan and layover for 36 hours then deadhead back to San Juan. The captain was Clyde Strong, one of my favorites.

We took off from San Juan with minimum fuel because the weather in Paramaribo was, as usual, clear and a million, but the company gave us an alternate airport, Georgetown, Guyana anyway, about an hour north. It was a nice flight, no thunderstorms along the way and airplane running smoothly. We cruised past Georgetown, our alternate, without giving it a second thought, I didn't even bother to check the weather. When we started descending into Paramaribo, the controller asked if we were ready to copy current weather. I rather nonchalantly picked up paper and pen and radioed back I was ready to copy.

"Paramaribo current weather is indefinite ceiling 100 feet, sky obscured, visibility 1/4 mile. Wind calm. What are your intentions?"

Boy talk about getting our attention, the flight engineer and I were now sitting on the edge of our seats. I was now asking about weather in Georgetown and the engineer was trying to firm up his fuel totals. Clyde was just leaning back in his seat, sipping on his coffee with a smirk on his face. Paramaribo stated they had no report of weather in Georgetown, "What are your intentions?"

The engineer reported just enough fuel to make it back to Georgetown but it would be close. Okay, time for the blank stare, I turned and looked at Clyde for guidance. He was still smiling and said, "Tell them we are going to land at Paramaribo, Mikey, I'll get us in alright."

Clyde briefed the ILS approach and proceeded to hand fly the airplane down the glide slope. I called off the altitudes while monitoring Clyde's approach, looking for any deviation from the localizer or the glideslope. There weren't any, not even a hint of one. As we descended through 200 feet, the normal minimums, I really started to sweat, it was so dark you couldn't see anything. At 100 feet the runway lights were barely glowing through the fog but by 50 feet you could finally make them out, they were right where they had to be and Clyde let the DC-8 touchdown firmly on the centerline. The engines roared into reverse thrust as Clyde slowed us to taxi speed and we turned off the runway and taxied to the gate.

I kicked myself for three days for being so lax and not checking Georgetown weather when we flew past, at least we would have known if we could have returned there. Without that knowledge, Clyde felt he had no choice but to land the airplane in that weather and he did it just right. That's why he was one of my favorite captains

Often, operations either neglected to file over-flight permits along your route or came up with some half-baked procedure and you had to either bluff your way through or come up with an alternate plan. There's nothing worse than flying at 33,000 feet and having Khartoum Control calling you and simply stating, "Big A 4615, rrrrreturn to base!!!"

He must have curled his "r" for 15 seconds, we just replied "STANDBY." That particular situation was resolved by us calling Miami Ops with the HF radio through Berna Radio on a phone patch. They also said "STANDBY," but did eventually come up with an over fly permit number for us.

Arrow Air DC-8-62 parks at passenger terminal at Gatwick Airport south of London, United Kingdom.

We used to gather around the airplane at Sigonella Naval Air Station in Sicily. We were flying a military "combo" charter (the front half of the cabin held cargo and the rear half had passengers). We were delivering everything to Diego Garcia in the middle of the Indian Ocean but had to make a fuel stop in Nairobi, Kenya. The first leg took up to seven hours 20 minutes. I believe the initial flight plan called for around 120,000 pounds of fuel. I would ask the First Officer how much fuel he thought we should load and he usually asked for 122,000 lb. but then the Flight Engineer would want to bump it up to 123,000 lb. We carried a mechanic with us on these flights and he flew along this route every week so when I asked him he said, "Not an ounce less than 128,000 pounds!" So, that is what we loaded onboard. The highest bidder always won.

Since this was a military charter we had a funky three letter identifier followed by a single digit for our call sign. We had been briefed by Miami Ops that since the Greeks didn't allow military over flights we should change our call sign to Big-A-123 and they would clear us right through. Yea, RIGHT! Actually it did work once, but generally they would not allow us through their airspace. We were filed with the military call sign and I'm sure we were handed off to them with that call sign. When we came up on frequency as Big-A-123 they wouldn't really be confused, they would start with the third degree.

"Big-A-123 is this a military flight?"

"Athens Control, Big-A-123 is a civilian aircraft, over!"

"Big-A-123, do you have military cargo and personnel aboard your aircraft?"

"Affirmative"

"Big-A-123, you must proceed via international waters!"

Proceeding via international water wasn't that big a deal as long as Muammar al-Gaddafi wasn't too upset with the U.S. At the time, Reagan hadn't ordered the bombing of his tent yet so we managed to sneak past every week. There is a thin line drawn along the Mediterranean Sea that separates Greek and Libyan airspace and we would be allowed to fly along that line. Every time this happened I would ask to turn right, direct to the International line but they would never allow that. We would have to turn around and exit their airspace where we entered. Now you understand why we carried the extra fuel each week.

About half way through the flight from Yakota, we would pass approximately 200 miles south of Anchorage, Alaska. The compass heading had swung from north to east southeast and it was decision time. If we had sufficient fuel to proceed to McChord Air Force Base and then fly to our alternate if the weather was too bad, we would continue. If for some reason our fuel burn was excessive, the weather forecast deteriorated at both airports, or some mechanical issue affecting our performance arose, we would land at Anchorage or Fairbanks and get more fuel. This is called a re-file flight plan. ATC knew you were going to McChord but you were actually only filed to Anchorage. We would notify the company we had sufficient fuel, re-file with ATC to McCord, and proceed. This evening, McCord visibility was dropping steadily but SEATAC was holding at two miles. Everything was looking good so we decided to carry on toward the foggy northwest.

Once we approached Egyptian airspace we would change back to the military call sign and proceed down the Nile River past Cairo and into Sudan. It was always a pain having to argue with Khartoum about our over flight permit. We would stay west of Ethiopia and then land in Nairobi for fuel. I'd ride in a rickety old VW bus across to the west side of the airport and pay the landing fees then back to the airplane. It was over a year of doing this before I ever saw Kenya in the daytime. The sun always set while we were over Sudan. From Nairobi we would head east toward Diego. That was a mere five-and-a-half-hour flight so by the time we began our descent the sun was searing holes in our eyes while we gulped black coffee and tried to keep each other awake.

The first time I flew to Diego Garcia was also right after I had upgraded to Captain in the DC-8. I had a good crew, but we were all anxious to see the island on descent. I kept saying, "I don't see any island, do you see an island?" There was a broken cloud layer so we wouldn't spot it until below it but it was fun to act concerned. It was their first time into Diego as well, if the island wasn't there, we had two hours of holding fuel and then we would go swimming. Two hours wasn't enough to reach anywhere but Diego.

Layovers in Diego Garcia were just long enough to get legal and catch a few hours sleep then go to the base liquor store for a bottle of Remy Martin. It only cost $5.00 for a liter of VSOP and a bottle never made it through the week layover back in Catania, Sicily.

Arrow Air DC-8 waiting to carry another load of charter passengers from the United Kingdom back to San Francisco or Los Angles, California.

We would have dinner in the Officers' Mess then ride the van to the airfield and get ready to head back to Sicily. Diego is on the exact opposite side of the globe from where I lived in Denver at the time so when it was midnight in Diego it was noon in Denver. I would usually want to call home on this flight and would wait until after Nairobi when it would be evening at home. Somewhere over the Sudan, the flight attendants had cooked these three pound baked potatoes and they would bring them up loaded with butter, sour cream, salt, and pepper. It was a feast for us and we looked forward to trying to polish these things off. Right after finishing mine for this evening, I tuned in Berna Radio and asked for a phone patch to my home. The operator took my credit card number and connected the call.

My wife, Charmian, answered and I enjoyed hearing the latest news from the domestic front then she asked if I would like to speak with our eight-year-old daughter Laura. When Laura came on, eventually she asked where I was, I told her we were at 35,000 feet above Sudan. It turns out she knew exactly where Sudan is since they were studying about it in school that very day. Unfortunately, what she knew most about Sudan was there were thousands of people starving because of the political instability below us. Her next question floored me, especially since I still had the remains of my three pound dinner in my lap, she said, "Oh my gosh dad, are you starving?" I assured her that I was not but the point was well taken, I had not given much thought about the suffering and turmoil a mere six miles below us until then. I've heard it called the 35,000 foot gap since then.

About an hour past Anchorage the eastern horizon would start glowing, finally hinting of the coming sunrise, and the stars began to fade. Sometimes Venus would suddenly appear. It would start to glow from red to blue to yellow, shining almost like a beacon just after it cleared the horizon. It was a stunning show and you almost couldn't believe it was a planet. The show would last four or five minutes then Venus turned to a steady white beam as it rose above the horizon. Soon we were radar identified with the Canadian ATC and no longer had to make position reports but we kept a sharp eye on the weather. Tonight Seattle was still reporting 400 foot overcast and two miles visibility but McChord had gone below minimums. The report read W 0 X, which meant, indefinite ceiling, visibility zero, sky obscured. We were not going to attempt an approach in that.

After working at Arrow Air for two years, one Friday afternoon in Denver I called the company to confirm my deadhead pass to San Francisco and my trip assignment to Guam. The crew scheduler informed me I had been removed from my trip by the Director of Operations. That didn't seem like good news. Very little good news came from the DO office. When I inquired what was up, the scheduler informed me I was to report Monday morning at Arrow Air Operations in Miami at 8 a.m. and I would start Captain upgrade school!

That took me by surprise. The boss at Arrow was adamant about not running a flight school and would only hire current and qualified crew members. The current chief pilot had managed to convince him his best option for covering the shortage of pilots for his expansion plans this summer was to promote within the ranks of the company. The pilots were also about to vote on ALPA union representation and that may have influenced this reversal of policy.

I was elated. Finally someone believed I could be a captain on a big airplane. I smiled all the way to Miami and then got down to business in ground school. I was in a class of ten first officers and as usual, I was the most junior. Also, I was the only pilot who had spent time as a flight engineer. I found out later, that was a big advantage. The ground school covered the bare minimum, if you didn't already know this stuff, you weren't going to get it in this ground school. I pitied the poor guys transitioning off of the 707. They didn't have a clue, even the guys who flew right seat on the DC-8 were having trouble understanding what was going on at the engineer's panel.

After three weeks we paired up and started the practice orals. The FAA would be over the next morning to start giving the real things. Being the most junior, I was paired with a 707 guy late in the afternoon, after everyone else completed their practice sessions. The instructor seemed agitated about something but he was fair with his questions and patient with us.

I was able to explain about every function of the DC-8 systems because I had managed them for two years as a flight engineer and knew them thoroughly. My poor partner was struggling, trying to remember what was taught in ground school and I tried to help him as much as I could but the instructor finally glared at me and told me to shut up for a while.

I was happy with my effort and the 707 guy said he thought he passed as well. I was still a little worried about the questions covering the ATP flying procedures while wandering around the world as an Airline Transport Pilot, we didn't cover any of that in the practice oral. I knew I was last man on the list and the Feds were only giving two orals a day so I would have several days to grill the guys coming out of their test about what I needed to study.

We gathered in the bar for an early bull crap session and compared notes on our experiences and most lamented about the lousy ground school. I went back to my room to pick up some extra beer money and noticed my message light blinking on the phone. It was the chief pilot, wanting me to call back immediately. When he answered my call he sounded relieved that I had gotten back to him so quickly. He informed me I needed to be in operations at 8 a.m. in the morning. They had cancelled all of the oral exams from the FAA except one since the examiner had already flown in just for these events. I was the only one they figured could pass the exam. The rest of the candidates would be back in ground school at 8 a.m. and it was my duty to inform them of this change as soon as I returned to the party. I wasn't too happy about that. Being first to take the exam wasn't what I wanted to do and informing the rest of my compadres wasn't a good way to make friends. They all breathed a sigh of relief after hearing the news. Plans were made to head to another bar to celebrate their reprieve but I hadn't been reprieved. I was under the gun the next morning so I left them to return to the room and study about ATP procedures.

About 200 miles north of McChord we were really sweating out the weather. McChord was still closed and Seattle was deteriorating. Seattle had gone from two miles visibility to one mile and the ceiling had dropped to 300 feet. We expected some deterioration as the sun came up but this was still before sunrise. We asked to hold just north of McChord to see if there was any improvement after sunrise. Now we really started to determine how much fuel was on board and I wanted to keep enough in reserve to divert up to Vancouver, Canada in case Seattle closed. Vancouver weather was excellent. The sun rose as we entered the hold and McChord stayed at zero visibility, Seattle started dropping to less than a mile. One turn in the holding pattern and we decided to divert to SeaTac before they also went to zero. The first officer set up the approach and we spotted the runway descending through 200 feet with about 3/4 mile visibility.

The oral was a piece of cake. The FAA examiner was recently furloughed from Braniff and had only flown 727s so he was new to the DC-8 as well. I had to teach him a few things about the fuel system and he was easily impressed so he gave me a passing grade and told the chief pilot that if the other candidates were as prepared as I was there would be no problems. I met my compadres for lunch and went over the oral questions with them and they all passed their exams the next week, after finishing the extra ground school. I was sent home to await my turn in the simulator; naturally I would be scheduled last due to my seniority. Over the following weeks I studied and practiced, flew a quick trip to Guam and back and agonized over the coming ordeal of the simulator check ride. When my turn finally came up, I struggled a little with the ADF approaches but finally passed the check ride from the FAA.

Next we were shipped to San Juan where we would meet the same FAA inspector who gave the orals for the airplane ride. Again I was the last to go. The inspector told me he had to catch a flight back to Miami that night and there might not be enough time to complete all of the check rides. I rode in the cockpit jump seat to watch the first pilot. He nailed the first ILS but his landing was so hard the whole airplane shook back and forth as we rolled out on the runway. From my seat I could see sweat start pouring down the back of his neck. I glanced back into the cabin at the eight other candidates and realized they were running up and down the aisle trying to stow the 50 or so passenger oxygen masks that had jarred loose on the touchdown. When I turned back around, the Fed was watching the same thing with a worried look on his face. The check captain cleaned up the airplane and we did a go-around. When I looked back in the cabin, everyone was sitting down again with grins on their faces trying to act like nothing happened. The Fed looked around again and just shook his head.

Everyone got to make a normal four engine ILS then the fun began. On the first go around the check captain pulled the throttle back on one engine. You had to go through the engine fail checklist on downwind, a pillow was placed in the windscreen in front of you, and your second approach was terminated with a three engine go-around. The third approach was a full stop landing still on three engines. After taxiing back to the departure end of the runway a new victim would get in the left seat and do it all over again. Everything went like clockwork, I could tell we were progressing through the check rides and I would get my turn with just enough time left for the inspector to catch his flight.

I did the takeoff normally and at 1,000 ft. engaged the autopilot on downwind. On base I clicked the autopilot off and turned onto the ILS. I came over the fence and flared for the landing but the only way we knew we touched down was when the spoilers deployed. It was literally the smoothest landing I'd ever done. We took off again and I re-engaged the autopilot but the check captain said the Fed wanted to see me hand fly the airplane. No sweat, I clicked it off and called for the engine failure checklist. The three engine approach and go around were uneventful and the last landing was another squeaker and we taxied back to the ramp.

The Fed started filling out the paperwork for our ATPs and type ratings as we all stood around grinning like damn fools. He finished up then left to catch the next jet back to Miami while we headed for the bar in the hotel. That was a big relief to get out of the way and we began to let off a little steam. Tom, the pilot I took the oral with, came over with a smile (he was always smiling) and stated to me, "Man, I'm glad you weren't the first pilot to go on the check ride."

I was the only one who actually made a decent landing. I didn't think too much about it though, when we hammered in on that first landing, I remembered when I took my airplane ride for the Flight Engineer rating five years previous, the guys had all made hard landings that day as well. None of them had any DC-8 time previous to then and the Feds can't expect you to be an expert at that point.

The next morning we boarded the plane back to Miami and the check captain told me to be in uniform and ready to fly all the way back to Denver with him. I figured he would be in the right seat but he insisted in riding in the jump seat and had the regular co-pilot in his seat. It was a nice flight to Denver and I counted off seven hours towards the required twenty-five hours of Initial Operating Experience (IOE). Two weeks later the Fed informed me, "Mike, it's clear to me you meet the minimum requirements to be an Airline Transport Pilot on DC-8s so I'll sign you off today."

Another stepping stone along the way, I was getting tired of constantly flying with a check airman as though I were getting a check ride on every flight but finally, after twenty-five hours I was signed off for Pilot-in-Command in the United States. I flew a few legs from Denver to San Juan and back then reported to Miami for my overseas check. That went alright, and now I could fly anywhere in the world as a captain on the old airplane.

After landing at SeaTac we taxied to the holding area on the west side of the runways to wait for the fog to clear at McChord. We were tired and cranky and ready to go to the hotel but couldn't do anything about it until we cleared US Customs and they were not going to drive across the airport just for us. We were begging for the fueler to come over and give us a little more gas to go to McChord but they were busy and said it may be over an hour before he would get to us. There is just nothing you can do about the situation when you've diverted to another destination and surprised everyone with your needs.

The mighty Douglas DC-8, one of the most beautiful aircraft ever built.

First Officer, Jim, got on the radio and started to vent his frustrations with the dispatcher, I sympathized with his anger but felt it best to rein him in a little. After all, you shouldn't be yelling at the guy who is going to schedule someone to come over to service you. Jim immediately remembered what he was doing and politely asked the dispatcher to send someone over as soon as possible. McChord weather was already improving and we were anxious to get there and into the hotel for a much needed rest.

I really enjoyed flying as a captain. I was, of course, scheduled with the most junior co-pilots because of my seniority. I was a little concerned about that until I started flying with these guys. Most of them came from commuter airlines and had been flying turboprops. I wasn't sure if I was up to teaching them how to fly DC-8s around the world but I didn't have to. These were literally some of the best instrument pilots I have ever flown with. Even though they had no jet experience, they had been fighting their way through the weather around the busy Northeast corridor for years and the transition to international flying was a piece of cake. Sometimes you would have to say something when they descended below 50 feet on landing, they were still figuring out how to land a jet. But most caught on right away and it was a privilege flying with these guys.

For the next two years I was caught up in the up and down cycle of charter flying. I was in the left seat for four months when some rule became effective banning those noisy DC-8s from all airports in the US except Stewart, 75 miles north of JFK. All of us new captains were sent back to the right seat and the new co-pilots back onto the streets. That got sorted out when someone figured out there weren't enough re-engined noisy airplanes to meet the needs of the military so all of a sudden it was okay to fly into JFK again and I was promoted back to the captain's seat. This happened three times in two years.

On the morning of December 12, 1985 I was in bed recovering from my last international foray when my wife, Charmian, woke me up. She said, "Mike, the news is reporting a DC-8 crashed this morning up in Canada!"

I jumped up wide awake and started firing questions at her as I put on my bath robe. On the way down the stairs she said she thought it was indeed an Arrow Air DC-8 and she didn't think there were any survivors. Quickly I began trying to remember who was flying the Canadian cargo contract that week. Unfortunately, the news just got worse and worse and then even worse as the morning progressed. This was absolutely the worst day in my life! It wasn't a cargo flight that crashed, it was a MAC flight with 248 servicemen returning from the middle east after their tour as peace keepers in the Sinai Desert. There were no survivors. For the rest of the day I sat in front of the TV, stunned at what had happened, I called crew scheduling to confirm who the crew on the fatal flight was and that really hit hard. It was the same crew I had flown with the previous week on this exact same flight.

No words can express the emotions and depression that followed this devastating morning. I was in shock for the next six months. The media furor that followed was demoralizing to the extreme. Arrow Air was crucified as the worst airline in the history of aviation. Every incident, every rumor of incident, and every lie a disgruntled furloughed pilot could make up was reported on the five o'clock news. The record of the captain killed that morning was dragged through the worst scrutiny I have ever seen. John was quite frankly the best DC-8 pilot I had ever flown with. Sometimes he was so particular about every detail of the flight it got to be a pain in the rear, but John was not departing until everything was in order. Whatever the reason for this crash, I knew it was nothing that John had done or left undone.

Two furloughed airline pilots came forward to be interviewed on the news. They stated they had been forced by Arrow Air management to fly unsafe airplanes. They said the maintenance was so bad at Arrow they weren't surprised one of the planes crashed. I was disgusted at these two prima donnas making statements like that, in the first place, I don't care who suggested they fly an unsafe airplane, how could they still be airline pilots after admitting they had complied and flown an unsafe flight! The maintenance at Arrow was not bad. If I called and reported a maintenance problem, it was fixed or deferred until it could be flown someplace where it could be addressed.

DAN RATHER REPORTING:

"ABC news today has learned that the Arrow Air DC-8 that crashed in Gander, Newfoundland last week was involved in two other narrow brushes with disaster. First was an aborted takeoff from Toledo, Ohio and the second was a tail strike taking off from Chicago O'Hare."

I was the captain when we aborted the takeoff in Toledo. Within a few minutes from that announcement, the phone rang, it was crew scheduling. The FAA requested that I and Richard Heisner (the captain flying the Chicago tail strike) be removed from all flying pending an investigation of the two incidents reported on ABC news. I was pretty upset, I had just been removed from a very lucrative flight to the Orient and there was no telling how long before I would be able to fly again. Frankly, I didn't have confidence that Arrow was going to survive this onslaught of negative publicity.

About six months prior to the accident I was assigned a flight from Toledo to Ramstein AFB in Germany. We loaded up the Ohio National Guardsmen and taxied out to the single runway. As I brought the throttles up for takeoff, engine number three began to backfire and I brought the throttles back to idle. We all knew what the problem was and the engine would run fine once it accelerated beyond a certain RPM but, there was no way I was going to take these guys to Germany without confirming that diagnosis. We taxied back after "the near brush with disaster," as reported by Dan Rather, and parked on the same ramp, I wrote the incident in the logbook and the engineer, who happened to also be a DC-8 qualified mechanic walked downstairs to open the cowling. He confirmed the PRC valve was stuck closed and fixed it. This valve was designed to open and relieve pressure inside the engine as it first accelerated to takeoff power then close after a few seconds. It was not unusual for it to stick shut once in a while. The engineer signed the logbook stating how he had addressed the incident, we called the company and related what had occurred and received another dispatch clearance to proceed.

It took the FAA about two weeks to figure this out and I was finally assigned the next flight to Yakota, Japan. Richard didn't fare so well. His incident happened when he brought the throttles up for takeoff and the airplane rocked back onto the tail skid. When he reduced power again the plane plopped back onto its nose and Richard taxied back to the hold short line. They realize the half-full airplane had been loaded with everyone in the rear, hence, when the low slung engines came up to power, the nose came up. He ordered everyone to move to the center of the airplane and then took off. They stopped at another airport and filled the airplane up then flew them all to their destination and ferried the airplane back to Miami. In Miami he wrote the incident in the logbook so an inspection of the tail skid could be accomplished, something he should have done in Chicago. He was suspended for six months for this transgression.

I began to fly as much as I could. I was losing more and more confidence in the company's survival. Just before leaving for Yakota I answered the home phone. It was a secretary for

Senator John Glenn's office. Senator Glenn was holding congressional hearings on the accident and he wanted me to come and testify about the unsafe conditions I observed while working at Arrow. He had the two airline pilots lined up to testify and wanted additional line pilots to bolster their testimony. I told them I would be glad to come to Washington and talk to Congress and here's is what I would have to say: "I have never been asked to and no one had ever even hinted to me that I should fly an Arrow Air airplane in a potentially unsafe condition. Furthermore, even if I had been asked, I would never agree to fly an unsafe airplane and anyone who would, even to save their job, should be violated by the FAA and should never be allowed into an airline cockpit again!"

The secretary was silent for a moment and then said, "Okay, Captain Larson, um, we'll get back to you on that." Naturally, I never heard from them again. They only wanted one thing said at the hearing, they had their own agenda.

The cause of the crash was never fully explained. Initially, the Canadian Safety Board determined that the airplane should have been de-iced before departure. There were airplanes being deiced on the ramp in Gander that morning but all of them had been on the airport overnight during some precipitation. Since the weather was clear when the Arrow airplane landed, John, the captain, did not feel a need for de-icing and rightfully so. This finding was later struck down by a CAB judge as preposterous and a new investigation was ordered. There was always a cloud of suspicion surrounding not only the crash but the reason for a quick determination. It was later documented that a high ranking Army officer ordered the crash site bull-dozed and covered within twenty-four hours of the accident. One theory in the final investigation about this is the fact that there had never been a successful terrorist attack in the Americas and no one wanted this to be the first. The fact that the aircraft was delayed in Cairo, Egypt for twenty-eight hours with all of the troops bags unloaded onto the ramp and then left unguarded was not revealed until over a year later. Also the Iran/Contra scandal became news about a year after the accident and some have tied that to the Arrow accident. Several eyewitnesses to the accident that day stated they observed fire streaming from the bottom of the DC-8 before it crashed, but they were not allowed to testify at the first hearing. Toxicology reports of smoke in the lungs of the deceased was also suppressed as that bit of information did not fit into the conclusion that the failure to de-ice caused the crash.

I was able to talk to an FAA investigator in Miami who had been present when they downloaded the information from the data recorder. He told me, "Everything was normal on takeoff until the airplane reached 75 feet and then everything just stabilized, it didn't accelerate, decelerate, descend, or climb for six seconds! At seven seconds the nose yawed to the right and the plane went down." The second investigation at least included most of this information in its final determination but they still would not call it a terrorist event and the cause of the crash is still just pure speculation. By the time that conclusion was published it was too late for Arrow. The disgruntled pilots did their deed at the congressional hearing, George Batchelor, Arrow Air's owner was grilled unmercifully by the Senators and Arrow filed Chapter 11 bankruptcy the next day.

The fueler finally pulled up under the wing and hooked up and added a couple of thousand pounds so we could fly to McChord safely. It cleared up at McChord and SeaTac so we started up and taxied out for takeoff. We landed at McChord, hustled through customs and, called the company to let them know we were heading for the hotel. Not so fast, they said. They needed the airplane in Oakland and wanted us to ferry it down there and leave it. There was no need to ask them why, we were told the company filed bankruptcy and all of the airplanes were being parked. We would be released in Oakland and needed to find our own way home from there. All Arrow Air crews were being furloughed as of the termination of our flight to Oakland. This was my last flight in a DC-8.

I guess, after seven years flying DC-8s you would think you would be used to being furloughed with a phone call by then. You don't though, because you still have house payments, children to feed and a wife to explain to why you wanted to be a jet pilot in the first place. I caught a ride on Frontier Airlines to Denver, the crew was very sympathetic with my plight and gave me a number to call in case they started hiring. At home I moped around for a week or so, watching the ongoing crucifixion of anything to do with Arrow Air. The company told us they were just reorganizing and would call us back to work as soon as they could but when my last paycheck bounced, I knew it was over, at least for me.

For two years I had been sitting on an application to New York Air given to me by a friend so I pulled it out and started filling out the information. I put it in the mail box and called George to tell him I was finally ready to change jobs. He was delighted and said to send the application in ASAP and he would see what he could do. I told him it was in the mailbox and I would wait to hear from them. Two hours later I got a call from the chief pilot's office asking me to come to an interview for a job on Wednesday.

The application I filled out was still in the mailbox out front, man, George works fast! This is the best thing that could have happened to me. I got the job at New York Air but it only lasted for eight months and we merged with Continental Airlines. Continental was in the process of expanding rapidly and was poorly managed at that time, but over the twenty years I worked there, it turned around and once again became a premier airline and a great place to work.

Author, Mike Larson, on retirement flight with Continental Airlines.

Continental was good to me, I have a decent retirement from them, thanks to ALPA, and I loved flying the 737 for them. It took twelve years before I regained the left seat again but I was always grateful for the job. Arrow did try to recall me during ground school at New York Air, but I refused.

They made it through the reorganization and eventually started flying MAC Charters again. They acquired newer and bigger airplanes, but never quite returned to the days when I worked for them.

Author, Mike Larson, flying his J-3 Cub.

I miss those pilots I flew with at Arrow. They were the best international pilots I've ever flown with and taught me how to fly a DC-8 around the world. I've benefitted tremendously over the years having been mentored by these guys and always applied what they taught me over the years flying for Continental. There is no doubt, going from jump pilot, to crop duster, to DC-8 flight engineer, to DC-8 Captain and finally captain at Continental Airlines has been quite a trip for me. I loved flying those jets around the country and the world but now that I'm retired and can look back on my experiences, I mostly only remember the good parts and find it hard to complain about some of the nonsense we had to put up with at times. I don't want to go back as it is quite frankly, hard work. Don't let anybody tell you an approach to minimums through an ice storm after midnight in Cleveland is fun. They don't pay you that kind of money for nothing, and just because you love your job doesn't make it any less of a job.

I am perfectly happy to be retired and fly my little J-3 Cub around our fly-in community, harassing the neighbors as I fly low past their houses every evening trying to get in as many touch and goes as I can before sunset. I have two granddaughters who visit us and they always ask to go for a ride in the Cub so I have a new job now. Grandfather!

Our beautiful daughter and two granddaughters.

Our son, Tristan and his beautiful wife Liz and my wife Charmian below.

ABOUT THE AUTHOR

Author, Michael D. Larson

My very first memory in life was one of airplanes. While playing in the front yard of our home on the Sioux City Air National Guard base housing I happened to look up and watch four silver airplanes in close formation fly down the runway and crisply peel off individually for landing. They were P-51 Mustangs flown by Air Guard pilots, my father may have been flying one of the airplanes, I'm not really sure.

When dad graduated from college we moved to Wichita, Kansas, where he worked for our family in grandpa's pest control business. He did not fly as pilot again. All of my uncles were still flying and I remember the day I realized I also wanted to be a pilot. I was probably five-years-old at the time and from that day on, even today; I want to be a pilot.

I began taking flying lessons at age fourteen, my first solo flight at age seventeen and still fly almost every day today at age sixty-eight. Like my good friend, Winn Baker (retired Delta Airline Captain) told me, "Mike, it's a good thing I know how to fly, because flying airplanes is all I know how to do!" That statement succinctly applies to me. I do not expect much to change in the future.

I managed to make a living with small airplanes for the first 15 years of my career and did eventually get an airline job and flew jets around the world for 27 years until I retired in 2006. In 1999, my wife Charmian and I decided to acquire our own airplane. That's where we began a wonderful journey of owning and flying a Cessna 195. I was familiar with this airplane; I flew one in the 70s so it was an easy decision over which type of airplane to buy. We were quite unprepared, for the onslaught of new friends we found in the form of the International Cessna 195 Club. They are a friendly group and each member is dedicated to preserving the "finest airplane Cessna Aircraft Company ever built." It has been a wonderful experience socializing with these people and learning from them the various nuances of flying and maintaining our 65-year-old Cessna 195.

It was in 1999, that I began writing about our experiences in our Cessna 195 and over the years I have written about my flying experience. I was encouraged to do this after finding several stories written by Charmian's mother in an envelope hidden in a drawer after her death. I knew immediately I had found a treasure and I also realized how important it is to a family history to document some of your own life experiences. For years I have wanted to do this book, but it wasn't until we found Trish Shapiro I was able to move forward on the project. Over the course of a few weeks, Trish has edited and formatted this effort and for that I am extremely grateful. So now, the job has been finished and I pass this book on to you to enjoy.

Michael D. Larson
Pilot

Made in the USA
Charleston, SC
28 June 2016